Bottomless Love

This Advent and Christmas, may our eyes be opened in new ways to God's deep, deep love for us, and may we be inspired to live more fully within it.

Not too far from our home (and a place we go for a walk after our Christmas Day service) is a lake called Gormire ('mire' is a Middle English word meaning swampy or boggy ground). One local legend has it that a village was drowned under the water after an earthquake; another claims that Gormire is a bottomless lake. I like to puzzle about what this means! Would I be able to visit Australia if I had the right diving kit? A bottomless lake is a concept I can't understand, but I find it compelling.

The idea that something can have no limit has an important theological significance for us, especially at this time of year. In the Christmas series of notes on Philippians we read of the 'descent' of Jesus in the incarnation: the eternal Word takes on human being with all the suffering and limitation that it entails – and he does it for us. Why would God put himself through that? Because he is Love, and there are no lengths or depths to which God will not go for his beloved creation. John 1:10 tells us that 'He was in the world, and though the world was made through him, the world did not recognise him'. This non-recognition is clear in our Luke readings, where we see how Jesus was marginalised and betrayed.

Love can be frightening *because of* its limitless character. Parents will sacrifice themselves for their children; friends will stand back and allow others to succeed, because of love. This is the Way to which we are all called if we follow Jesus. It demands everything from us but, if we all practise love, then we are also given everything we need by others. Imagine a world in which that is so – imagine the global economy, the environment, the world health policies. The coming of Jesus in Bethlehem opens our eyes to the possibilities and the challenge; and when he comes again, it will be so.

Sally Nelson
Editor

Annabel Moule
Content Assistant

ON THE COVER: '...the Old Testament ends and the voice of prophecy falls silent. We turn the page and read: 'This is the genealogy of Jesus the Messiah'... '

Image credit: Shutterstock / laurenshin

The Writers

MARY EVANS is a former theological lecturer, still involved with research supervision and marking. Writing, speaking, church family, friends and Langham Partnership Board responsibilities fill much of the rest of her available time.

PETER S C POTHAN has been in full-time Christian work as a theological teacher and writer since 1972. He was an Academic Consultant at the Global School of Open Learning in Bangalore, India. He is retired and lives in Bangalore with his wife, children and grandchildren.

PHILIP CHURCH formerly taught biblical studies and remains involved with research supervision and marking, and teaching in majority-world countries. He is a board member of A Rocha Aotearoa, NZ. He and his wife, Dorothy, have three children and four grandchildren.

JOHN HARRIS is Senior Biblical Consultant for Bible Society Australia. In active retirement he continues his involvement in the translation of the Bible into indigenous aboriginal languages. John is married to Judith and they have three children and six grandchildren.

STEPHEN TRAVIS taught New Testament studies for many years at St John's College, Nottingham. His most recent book is a major revision of *Exploring the New Testament: Letters and Revelation* (SPCK)

JOE KAPOLYO comes from Zambia. He is married to Anne, and they have two daughters and three grandchildren. In 2017, Joe retired from 41 years of full-time Christian ministry, which included SU youth work, three pastorates and twelve years as a theological educator.

PETER MORDEN is Senior Pastor of Cornerstone Baptist Church Leeds and Distinguished Visiting Scholar, Spurgeon's College, London.

SALLY NELSON is the Dean of Baptist Formation at St Hild College, Yorkshire, UK, where she also teaches Christian doctrine and pastoral care. She is a Baptist minister and has been the commissioning editor for *Encounter with God* since 2015.

ANNABEL MOULE is a Content Assistant at Scripture Union and the content manager for *Encounter with God*. She studied English Literature at Oxford Brookes University and Theology at the University of Oxford.

Contents

Scripture Union is a member of the worldwide Scripture Union international community.
Website: https://scriptureunion.global

BACK TO THE BEACH!

How we have missed having holidays and missions in person! Thanks to your faithful support and with the efforts of many amazing volunteers, in summer 2021, hundreds of young people encountered the God who loves them.

SU Mission Enabler Toby Chant, together with others from the South West Regional Team, took on running Polzeath Family Mission when former leaders Alison Withers and Matt Smith stepped down after many years of faithful service.

Planning the mission had its challenges. Toby says, 'Covid constraints were constantly changing back then. In the end, we decided the safest thing was to make our plans using the existing restrictions, in the hope that restrictions would have loosened by the time of the mission itself.

'The biggest issue was having a team half the usual size, because we needed to keep them socially distanced and in bubbles. That meant we could only accommodate around 12 people instead of the usual 30. Also, half of that much reduced team was new. Thankfully, the other half really knew the ropes, for which we were so grateful to God!'

Making connections; building relationships

The usual centrepiece of Polzeath Family Mission is the Road Show, a broadcast of the gospel from a stage. However, this would have risked drawing a crowd which the team considered to be unwise at that point of the pandemic. They would have to adapt. Fortunately, Toby is no stranger to innovation.

'We set up sports and activities in small groups spread out across the beach: volleyball, football, tennis, building sand marble runs and so on. Most afternoons over a hundred children, young people and families took part. This worked really well actually, as we wanted to focus on children and young people without a church connection. Having a variety of activities meant our team were able to chat with individual children and bring faith into the conversation more naturally.

... our team were able to chat with individual children and bring faith into the conversation more naturally.

'One interesting aspect of Polzeath is that almost all those who visit the mission are visitors rather than locals. But they're not one-off visitors. Most of the children and young people come with their families to Polzeath for the same week or fortnight every year, staying at the same guest house or in the same caravan. So the great thing is that this summer we'll be able to build on the relationships we developed with the same children and young people who came last year.'

So open to exploring faith

Each day started with Bible-based sessions for three different age groups. Toby says, 'Initially, most of the children and young people coming to those sessions were from Christian families. Then, as we got to know other children we met at the beach activities, we invited them to come along too. And because they had been playing volleyball or doing other activities alongside the kids from Christian families, it was quite comfortable for them to take that step. So the numbers grew during the week – by the end we had up to 15 children or young people in each group.

'Many of these children without church connections were so open to exploring faith. In one group, we discussed the day of Pentecost in one of the sessions and offered to pray for children individually. The new youngsters wanted prayer too – actually, they had a real hunger for it! On another day, we discussed God's forgiveness. We invited the kids to take a stone from the beach, pray for forgiveness, and then throw the stone far out into the sea as a sign that God would remember their sins no more. The children without church links took part

just as enthusiastically as those from Christian families. It's not for me to say that they're now on a journey of faith, but they were clearly very receptive.

'Then there were the two lads that our intern, Matt, met on the beach one afternoon. He was playing football with them and they were chatting together. It turned out that they came from Bristol and one of them had a connection to one of our other team members. Matt was about to set up a football project in Bristol, so he gave them his details and invited them to contact him when they'd got back home and get involved. And they did! So Matt now has an opportunity to build a relationship with them on their shared home turf, which is great!'

Learning to share faith boldly

Taking part in the Polzeath Family Mission team really benefited Josh, Matt and Ydson, the three SU trainees.

Toby says, 'When I asked Josh what he thought the biggest benefit was of being on Polzeath Family Mission team, he said that now he had more self-confidence in stepping out and sharing his faith with complete strangers. He said that on his way home, after the mission, he'd dropped in to see a friend. They had gone for a drink and got talking to a stranger in the pub. It ended up with them praying for him – and Josh's friend says that this man has been going to her church ever since. 'Some weeks later, Josh phoned the family of a young man who didn't turn up at another of our projects one day, to check if everything was all right. It turned out that the mum was poorly, and so Josh prayed for them over the phone. The mum was so grateful that she was in tears.'

Discovering that God is real

The team were also able to strengthen links with Tubestation, the local beachside church which doubles as a café and art gallery. A Tubestation volunteer was on the Mission team, and the Bible-based sessions for older teenagers took place in the church garden.

God is real and present,
here and now.

It was there that Tubestation hosted a barbecue one night. Toby recalls, 'They had an impromptu worship session. As I looked around at all the young people, I saw this lad James, who is in his early teens. We'd met him on the beach and invited him to the Bible sessions and he'd come along every single day. Now here he was, absolutely transfixed, with his eyes closed as he drank in the words and music of the worship songs – perhaps discovering for the first time that God is real and present, here and now.

'We can't wait until July, and the chance to reconnect with James and the many other children and young people we met last year. We look forward to journeying with them as they explore faith, encounter God and find in him true purpose for their lives.'

A shorter version of this story first appeared in *Connecting You*, SU's free quarterly supporter magazine, in winter 2021. If you'd like to receive copies of *Connecting You* and learn more of how God is moving in the hearts and lives of children and young people today, you can sign up online at su.org.uk/connectingyou.

Using this Guide

Encounter with God is designed for thinking Christians who want to interpret and apply the Bible in a way that is relevant to the problems and issues of today's world. It is based on the NIV translation of the Bible, but can easily be used with any other version.

Each set of readings begins with an *Introduction* to the section you are about to study. The *Call to Worship* section at the start of each note should help you consciously to come into God's presence before you read the passage. The main *Explore* section aims to bring out the riches hidden in the text. The *Growing in Faith* section at the end suggests ways of applying the message to daily living.

The *Bible in a Year* readings at the foot of the page are for those who want this additional option.

DAVID:
A HERO WITH FLAWS

The book of 2 Samuel records Israel's history during David's reign. This section records a series of incidents in the latter section of that reign, concentrating largely but not exclusively on David's leadership. However, they are not just accurate accounts of past events. Like all Scripture, these stories are 'God-breathed and ... useful for teaching, rebuking, correcting and training in righteousness'.[1] We should read the chapters not just observing what happened, but also asking what we are meant to be learning and why, given the inevitable limitations on space, the author has chosen to include these particular stories.

Each day we can only concentrate on a few verses, but the account is not just a collection of individual stories but a carefully composed book. We should therefore be looking out for ongoing concerns and interests that arise, asking what this very gifted author is intending us to learn, how he expects us to feel and what difference it might make to the way we live our lives for God.

The chapters convey a real sense of affection and appreciation of David, but there seems to be a special concern for pointing out his weaknesses and failures. It is possible that the writer is reflecting on 1 Samuel 13:14 and asking whether David really was the one God sought, who was 'after his own heart'. David as psalmist fits this picture well, but the stories we shall read do raise doubts about David as king! Look out, too, for the way David interacts with others, his attitude to keeping promises, his treatment of his family, his close but strained relationship with Joab – and maybe for other ongoing themes not mentioned here.

Mary Evans

---

[1] 2 Tim 3:16   [2] Acts 13:22

2 Samuel 22:17–30

The God who Sees

'She gave this name to the Lord who spoke to her: "You are the God who sees me," for she said, "I have now seen the One who sees me."'[1]

David understood clearly here, at the beginning of his reign, that the unchanging God supported him, brought him through difficulty, saw and knew him. It wasn't until later that he became more aware of his own potential for sin, and the reality of God's forgiveness. Unlike his claim to righteousness in today's passage (v 21), in Psalm 103:10 (continuing the repentance seen in Psalms 32 and 51) he proclaimed that God 'does not treat us as our sins deserve or repay us according to our iniquities'. David's confidence in God never changed but his confidence in himself did! In today's chapter, he believed he had followed and obeyed God in every way, and would be honoured for it. He happily proclaimed that God treats everyone according to their 'righteousness' (vs 21,25) – fully trusting that he was righteous and would be treated well.

I can empathise with David! As a young Christian whose belief in my own faith and faithfulness was strong, I would probably have been happy to recite this psalm with confidence. In later years I struggle, as I think David too would have done, with some of the words here. However, God has not changed – he is still our 'lamp' who turns our 'darkness into light' (v 29). The difference for Christians is that we can confidently speak of God's faithfulness to the faithful, not because of any righteousness of our own but because of the perfect righteousness of Christ that has been accounted to us. Paul explains clearly in Romans 3 and elsewhere that, although all (including David!) have sinned, 'righteousness is given through faith in Jesus Christ to all who believe'.[2] So, the strong 'Wow' that comes out so clearly from David here can still be our 'Wow', as forgiven sinners.

Read this passage aloud, speaking loudly when it speaks of God and quietly when it proclaims the writer's innocence. Then thank God for the righteousness that we have in Christ.

[1] Gen 16:13 [2] Rom 3:22

BIBLE IN A YEAR: **Isaiah 61,62; Hebrews 12**

The God who Provides

'Fear not, I am with you, so be not dismayed; I am your God and will come to your aid: I'll strengthen you, help you and cause you to stand.'[1]

It seems appropriate that we have been assigned this psalm to consider in the midst of David's psalm in 2 Samuel 22. Here, too, David looks at God in the context of looking at himself, but the view of himself is so different! Here we have moved from 'I have been blameless … The LORD has rewarded me according to my righteousness'[2] to an awareness of being 'overwhelmed by sins' (v 3) and of being rewarded only because of God's grace and forgiveness. I don't have any problem reciting this psalm with confidence! David's wholehearted praise for God and the thankful presentation of God's character comes here from a humble awareness of his own sinfulness and a grateful acknowledgement that he doesn't deserve the privilege of being chosen by God and able to live close to God 'in your courts' (v 4).

In that context, what do we learn of God? We see that he demands integrity and obedient service (v 1). He answers prayer and welcomes all (v 2). We can't be sure whether David understood fully just what that 'all' implies, but 'the hope of all the ends of the earth' (v 5) certainly shows some awareness. God's deeds are 'awesome and righteous' (v 5) – with the implication that as he is 'our Saviour' and 'hope' we too have a responsibility to reflect him in our righteous deeds. Verses 9–13 speak of God's deep concern for his creation; again the implication is that we too have a responsibility to cherish and care for this wonderful world that God has provided for us. The world is coming to a realisation of just how important that is, although one is saddened by the realisation that it took the knowledge of impending disaster for us to begin to take any real notice or any real action.

Lord, you have provided for us in so many ways. Help us to care for others and for your whole creation, reflecting your care and your provision.

[1] Author unknown, published by J Rippon, 1787 [2] 2 Sam 22:24,25

BIBLE IN A YEAR: Isaiah **63,64; Hebrews 13**

2 Samuel 22:31–51

The God who Enables

'The LORD is my strength and my shield; my heart trusts in him, and he helps me. My heart leaps for joy, and with my song I praise him.'[1]

At this stage in his life David might have been overconfident in his own blamelessness (v 24) but there is no doubt that he understood that any abilities he had were given by God. It is God who is his Rock, providing strength and refuge when fleeing from the enemies spoken about in verse 1. God enables him to run safely on the heights, like a mountain deer, but also provides a safe path when his ankles are in danger of giving way. God delivers, preserves, avenges, sets free, exalts and rescues. It is God who fully deserves all the praise that David can give him.

It is never easy to work out the exact relationship between the work God does for us and the work he expects us to do. David had to fight battles, climb mountains, lead armies, walk the walk; but he could not have done it without God. God was always there helping and guiding, but the work itself had to be done by David. He could not just sit back and let God get on with it. At times it was doing just that that got him into trouble! Many years ago, I met a student coming out of an exam who said, 'Well, I managed OK in the first half, but the second half I had to leave to God'. I was very tempted when giving the paper back to write, 'Well, your bit wasn't too bad, but the bit you say God did, was very poor!' Depending on God was not an excuse for not having done any revision! Like David, we must get on and do the work God has given us, but we must be very clear that it is God who enables us to do so.

Talk with a friend about times when you were aware of God working with you and for you – and times when you never thought about God's help behind the scenes.

[1] Ps 28:7

BIBLE IN A YEAR: **Isaiah 65,66; John 1**

A Personal Epitaph

'For me to live is Christ, to die is gain … There is no peace, no joy, no thrill, like walking in his will, for me to live is Christ.'[1]

This is most likely a prepared final statement, rather than David's actual 'last words' (v 1): a message that he wants everyone, particularly his own descendants, to hear. Our 'last wills and testaments' tend to concentrate on how our material possessions should be distributed, but maybe we should recapture the tradition of making a statement of what we want our heirs to know! Notably, David writes as 'son of Jesse' (v 1), as the 'man' not as the king. He is aware that he is 'the hero of Israel's songs' (v 1) but he wants them to remember his Spirit-inspired words, rather than any actions. Parallelism, saying the same thing twice in different ways, was a common method of emphasis; and in verse 2 we have more parallelism, to make doubly sure that his readers understood the importance of God's words. God, David's Rock in his youth and still in his old age, has spoken.

The message itself is short and simple: any ruler who 'rules in the fear of God' (v 3) brings tremendous blessing, like 'light of morning' or 'brightness after rain' (v 4). In verse 5 it may look as if David returns to the brash confidence of his youth – God has blessed me, so my house must be righteous, – but at this stage of his life he knows he doesn't deserve God's blessing.[2] The point is that it is by God's grace that he has been made right with God. The covenant has been given[3] and David's descendants have no excuse for failure. However, he knows only too well that any individual descendants could exclude themselves by not ruling 'over people in righteousness' (v 3); any such will 'be cast aside like thorns' (v 6) and their reign will bring as much blessing as a thorn bush to a farmer.

Lord, help me to live so that people will be blessed as by 'brightness after rain' and to leave a legacy of the knowledge of you as the Rock.

[1] Keith White, 'For me to Live is Christ' [2] Ps 103:10 [3] 2 Sam 7

BIBLE IN A YEAR: **Jeremiah 1,2; Psalms 112,113**

2 Samuel 23:8-23

The Supporting Cast

'For my Father's will is that everyone who looks to the Son and believes in him shall have eternal life, and I will raise them up at the last day.'[1]

Be honest! How often, when you are faced with lists of names within Scripture, do you skip past without reading them and only pause when you reach another specific story? However, these lists and names are significant. This chapter reminds us that no leader stands alone; each depends on the advice and support of many others. Our reading ends at verse 23, but the whole chapter is worth skimming through! We see here warriors, just as brave and wise, just as much used by God, as David was. We can't be sure whether the 'Three' and the 'Thirty' were general terms, or limited groups, only adding new members when one died. We do know that these were significant people, known to God and deserving recognition by God's people. They came from different tribes, clans and areas. Some, like Uriah the Hittite, came from immigrant families. Some have been previously acknowledged but many are new to us, a reminder that not all God's actions within Israel are recorded. It is notable that Joab is not on the list, only mentioned in the identification of his brothers, and that the list finishes in verse 39 with Uriah, probably to draw attention to David's failures. (In the parallel list in 1 Chronicles 11, Uriah's name comes much higher up.)

Amid these lists is the story of David's thirst and the way in which his loyal followers risked their lives to fetch him a drink from his well-remembered special well! David's act of pouring out the water instead of drinking it might be seen as wasteful or disrespectful, but in fact it was honouring. Their gift was so special that it was worthy of being offered to God as a drink offering, which usually would have been the finest wine.

Lord, help us never to ignore the 'Threes' and the 'Thirties' who serve within our communities but to recognise how many people you use to bring about your 'great victories'.

[1] John 6:40

BIBLE IN A YEAR: **Jeremiah 3,4; John 2**

2 Samuel 24:1–17

Crime and Punishment

'For it is by grace you have been saved, through faith – and this is not from yourselves, it is the gift of God'.[1]

This chapter raises difficult questions! If it was God who 'incited David' (v 1) why was God so clearly annoyed with what he did? And what was so wrong with counting the people, when it had been done many times before without ill effect? In the parallel account in 1 Chronicles 21, it is Satan who incites David. Maybe our writer is emphasising God's ultimate sovereignty over all things. It is not clear what David thought God meant, but it is clear that, for some reason, what he actually did was wrong! Maybe God was challenging David to think more clearly about what the God he had been learning to know might really want. Micah 6:6–8 might assist our thinking here. Maybe the key is that David was supposed to count the whole people and he only counted 'the fighting men' (v 2), implying that it was the army, not God, on which David was depending to keep Israel safe. Militarism, with an excessive emphasis on armies and weapons, has been a real danger to many societies throughout history. It is interesting that at this point it was Joab who seems to have had a better understanding of God's desires than David! Was David deliberately ignoring Joab's advice because of their previous history?

The interrelationship between the community and its leaders here is clear. God was angry with Israel; David was the one taking sinful action, against advice, but as with Saul's sin described in chapter 21, all Israel suffered because of this. Ironically, in this case, so many people died, presumably including many soldiers, that the census was no longer valid! The punishment, on David and on the people, was deserved, but the story ends with further evidence of God's mercy, stressing the fact that we don't always get what we fully deserve!

It is often said 'a people get the leaders they deserve'. How far do we think this is true? What should Christians in a democracy look for when they vote?

[1] Eph 2:8

BIBLE IN A YEAR: **Jeremiah 5,6; John 3**

2 Samuel 24:18–25

The End of the Matter

'The end of all things is near. Therefore be alert and of sober mind so that you may pray. Above all, love each other deeply'.[1]

This last section of 2 Samuel tells us about the end of David's reign, finishing with a story of astute negotiation, commitment to God and the recognition and final taking up of his own responsibility. 1 Kings follows on directly, beginning with David at the end of his life having lost the ability to carry out further responsibilities or even to care for himself. The four books of Samuel and Kings belong together, but the writer apparently wants us to look back over David's reign and, even while clearly aware of weaknesses and failures, also to see David's strengths and successes. We have a lovely picture here of eastern negotiations, where it is hard to know when a suggestion, such as Araunah's offer to provide everything, is genuine or just part of the cultural power play. In either case, David wanted to be very clear that he accepted his responsibility.

This was his offering, his sacrifice, acknowledging both his own sin and his own thankfulness to God. 1 Samuel began with worship and sacrifice offered at God's house in Shiloh[2] and 2 Samuel ends with worship and sacrifice at what was to become the site of the new Temple.[3]

The account ends with a repetition of the statement made at the end of the story of the consequences of Saul's sin.[4] God 'answered his prayer on behalf of the land' (v 25). The writer has been consistently clear that sin has consequences and must be dealt with but, once it is dealt with, life moves on. God is still listening, still caring, still powerful, still answering. The next stage of Israel's history may be worse or may be better but, at this point, hope remains.

Lord, help us to take responsibility for our failures. Thank you that you are a God of mercy and hope, allowing us to move on. Help us do that too.

[1] 1 Pet 4:7,8 [2] 1 Sam 1:3 [3] 2 Chr 3:1 [4] 2 Sam 21:14

BIBLE IN A YEAR: **Jeremiah 7,8; Psalms 114,115**

ADVICE ON PASTORSHIP

The two epistles to Timothy and that to Titus are known as Paul's 'pastoral epistles'. They are letters of instruction to Timothy and Titus, about their pastoral duties in Ephesus and Crete. Paul wrote them in his old age, after his release from captivity in Rome. As well as teaching on Christian leadership, the pastorals provide a mature insight into Paul's last days. He instructs Timothy and Titus on handling the problems they encounter in the oversight of their churches and he sets out the qualities they should look for in appointing church leaders. He gives advice on personal conduct. Timothy was not naturally brave, and he was often unwell. He needed encouragement. Paul's confidence, however, was not misplaced. He talks warmly of his 'son in the faith'.[1]

Second Timothy is Paul's last and most moving letter. After a lifetime of service and suffering for Christ, he is in prison once more and longs to see Timothy. He instructs Timothy as a young Christian leader and charges him to hold fast to the sound teaching of the gospel. It is difficult to dispute the authorship because of the abundance of personal notes. Paul asks Timothy to come to him and bring Mark and the books and cloak Paul left in Troas. He warns him about heresies affecting the churches and encourages him to preach the Scriptures and to promote godly living and spiritual perseverance. He concludes with his own epitaph: 'I am already being poured out like a drink offering, and the time for my departure is near. I have fought the good fight, I have finished the race, I have kept the faith' (4:6,7).

While you study this letter, try to see what lessons you can find for your church and your ministry.

Peter S C Pothan

FOR FURTHER READING

John Stott, *The Message of 2 Timothy*, Bible Speaks Today, IVP, 1973
Craig S Keener, *The IVP Bible Background Commentary: New Testament*, IVP, 1993
Luke Timothy Johnson, *The Writings of the New Testament*, SCM Press, 1986

[1] 1 Tim 1:2; cf Acts 16:1,2; 2 Cor 1:1; Phil 1:1

2 Timothy 1:1–7

Blessed to be a Blessing

Praise God for the blessings he has given you in those who first shared Jesus with you and your new life in him.

In his first letter, Paul greeted Timothy as 'my true son in the faith'.[1] Here his greeting is 'my dear son' (v 2), showing his warm affection for his young convert and colleague. Paul 'constantly' remembers Timothy in his prayers (v 3).[2] He must have had a large heart to carry such a loving concern for so many people. 'Long' (see v 4) is a word expressing intense desire. In Paul's letters we see his real humanity. He was a stalwart soldier, but he had a tender heart. Do we pray regularly for others?

Timothy had a godly mother and grandmother. His father was Greek and presumably an unbeliever, his mother Eunice was a believing Jewish woman who became a Christian. His grandmother Lois had evidently been converted, for Paul talks of the 'sincere faith' of all three generations (v 5). These godly women had instructed Timothy out of the Old Testament so that from childhood he had 'known the Holy Scriptures'.[3] Timothy is urged to 'fan into flame the gift of God' (v 6) given to him when Paul laid his hands on him. This would most naturally be taken as the time of Timothy's ordination. Are you aware of your God-given gifts? Are you using them in his service?

Paul reminds Timothy that God has not given us a spirit of timidity or cowardice, but a spirit of power, of love and of self-discipline (v 7). The effective Christian worker must have the power of the Holy Spirit, but that power must be expressed in a loving spirit or it may do damage. Be strong in the Spirit in your life and ministry.

Thank God that you have been blessed with every spiritual blessing in heavenly places in Christ Jesus.[4]

[1] 1 Tim 1:2 [2] Cf Rom 1:10; 1 Thess 1:2; 3:6 [3] 2 Tim 3:15 [4] Cf Eph 1:3

BIBLE IN A YEAR: **Jeremiah 9,10; John 4**

Praising God in Public

'Praise our God, all peoples, let the sound of his praise be heard'.[1]

This is a wonderful song, as the psalmist praises God for all he has done for the nation. Let us also praise him for all he has done in the past. We may not have had to cross the Red Sea on dry ground, but if we try to remember we will realise how many of our Red Seas and problems he has helped us through. God is always good to us and the miracles and guidance in the past have led to all we have become today.

Looking back at my life I can see how God blessed and protected me. When I was one year old and my sister was two, my mother was driving us in the mountainous roads in the Nilgiri Hills in South India. The brakes failed and we nearly went off the cliff, but God protected us. My sister became a missionary doctor and I a Bible teacher. I was led to Christ by the Scripture Union General Secretary, Cecil M Johnson, when I was ten years old and God called me for the next 20 years, though I ran away. When I finally followed him at the age of 31, I realised that he had been training me for the ministry those years in my secular work. God has blessed me in these past 50 years of ministry and has taken me to preach around India and abroad. He has helped me to write many theological study books and I have mentored thousands of students, all through the grace of God.

Praise God for all the blessings in your life. How has he led and protected you? Like Timothy, praise God for your godly family, if you had one, and the upbringing you had. God is always worthy of praise, and we should make the effort. Finally, praise God for your nation and its leaders.

'Praise be to God, who has not rejected my prayer or withheld his love from me!' (v 20).

[1] Ps 66:8

BIBLE IN A YEAR: **Jeremiah 11,12; John 5**

2 Timothy 1:8–18

Be Faithful

God blessed us, saved us and called us to serve him. Are we faithful?

Paul's personal testimony (vs 8–12) begins with a confession that God saved him and called him 'to a holy life' (v 9). The next part of this verse picks up his central theme in Romans: 'not because of anything we have done but because of his own purpose and grace ... given us in Christ Jesus'. Grace is central to his theology; only through grace can we be united with Christ. This hidden grace has now been revealed to the human race 'through the appearing of our Saviour, Christ Jesus' (v 10). At his first coming, Christ destroyed death through his own death on the cross.[1] Paul was appointed 'a herald and an apostle and a teacher' (v 11) and his preaching of the gospel had cost him much in suffering and persecution, but he trusted in the God who called him.

Paul admonishes Timothy to keep the 'pattern of sound teaching, with faith and love in Christ Jesus' (v 13). Doctrine is to be lived and proclaimed with faith and love. Paul had entrusted preaching and teaching to Timothy. This goal could not be accomplished in one's own human strength, but only 'with the help of the Holy Spirit who lives in us' (v 14). Are you guarding what God has given you?

Paul laments his desertion. Those must have been lonely hours for the aged apostle in prison, facing almost certain death and forsaken by his friends. It is difficult for us to understand why God's servants, who have given themselves in sacrificial service to others, should suffer like this at the end – but Paul knew that the glory of the next life would repay it all. Pray for Indian missionaries and others who are working alone in tribal areas and often feel alone and deserted, that God will comfort them and encourage them in his strength.

Lord, help us to be faithful and guard what you have entrusted to us.

[1] Cf Heb 2:14

BIBLE IN A YEAR: **Jeremiah 13,14; John 6**

Strong in God's Grace

'… just as you received Christ Jesus as Lord, continue to live your lives in him … strengthened in the faith as you were taught, and overflowing with thankfulness.'[1]

Paul exhorts Timothy to 'be strong in the grace that is in Christ Jesus' (v 1). How can one be strong in grace? Grace means undeserved favour. Just as we are saved by grace,[2] so we must live by grace.[3] This means trusting completely in Christ and his power, not trying to live in our own strength alone.

Paul then sounds his frequent note about preserving and transmitting the truth.[4] Paul had entrusted the gospel to Timothy, and Timothy must pass it on to other teachers. If the church consistently followed this example, it would expand rapidly, as believers learned to teach others and commission them, in turn, to teach others. In the great commission, Jesus asks us to make and teach disciples.[5] Unfortunately, some foreign missionaries in India made converts, not disciples, who were dependent on them for everything. Today we teach that the local church should not only be self-governed and self-supporting, but also self-propagating. In North East India the Ao Nagas and the Mizos began to go out after the harvest and share the gospel in other villages. After 10 years, there were no more unconverted Ao Nagas or Mizos and so they turned to other tribes.

Paul uses three pictures of the Christian life. First, the *soldier* (vs 3,4): 'endure hardship'[6] suggests pain and suffering as part of the Christian's lot in life. That will inevitably happen as we engage in warfare against evil. Second, the *athlete* (v 5): Paul is fond of athletic metaphors. Christians must be good spiritual athletes. The goal of an athlete is to 'receive the victor's crown', but only if an athlete competes 'according to the rules'. Third, Paul speaks of the *farmer* (vs 6,7): pastors must sow the seed and cultivate. Paul emphasises hard work and diligence.

Lord, help us to be strong and faithful in ministry.

[1] Col 2:6,7 [2] Eph 2:8,9 [3] Rom 6:14 [4] Cf 2 Tim 1:13,14 [5] Matt 28:16-20 [6] New King James version

BIBLE IN A YEAR: **Jeremiah 15,16; Psalm 116**

2 Timothy 2:14–19

Workers Approved by God

Lord, help us to be strong in biblical doctrine and not moved by wrong teaching around us.

Paul now emphasises the solid foundation of truth (v 19), understood as the teaching of Jesus[1] and his apostles[2] or, more widely, the church.[3] Paul assures us that God knows those who are his, and that they know the Lord and are called to holiness.[4] Good doctrine is basic to Christian life: we need to handle the Word of truth well (v 15). To do this we must study the Word of God. There are false teachers in the world today, as in Timothy's time, and if we are not strong in the Word we can easily be swayed. One prevalent heresy is the 'prosperity gospel', which is enticing in the affluent West and even for middle-class Christians in India. We should be awake and vigilant.

Paul gives three warnings. First, avoid 'godless chatter' (v 16); second, do not get involved in foolish arguments because such arguments are confusing, useless and even harmful. False teachers can argue about unnecessary details and cause strife and division. Third, Paul asks us to ignore unbiblical teaching, such as speculation about the resurrection (vs 17,18). In January 2020, one so-called prophet said in his New Year message that 2020 would be a year of great blessings and peace, but now we know it was the era of the Covid-19 virus.

We need to study the Bible carefully and be aware of false teaching. When I studied at a liberal college in Bangalore, I decided to try to prove my evangelical faith, for if it was false I was a fool to hold on to it. I applied logical thinking to my studies and came to two conclusions. First, the Bible was logical and true; and second, that some Christians based too much thinking on conjecture and baseless theories. I became a stronger evangelical!

Help us, Lord, to be approved workers for God, correctly handling the Word of truth.

[1] See 1 Cor 3:11 [2] See Eph 2:20; Rev 21:14 [3] 1 Tim 3:15 [4] Cf 2 Tim 1:9

BIBLE IN A YEAR: **Jeremiah 17,18; John 7**

Consecrated for God

We need to be consecrated vessels for God, to be used by him.

In verses 20 and 21 Paul urges Timothy to be the kind of person Christ could use for his noblest purposes. For this he uses the examples of vessels in a large house, of different kinds and materials for different purposes. Paul has often pointed out that all Christians are important and all have their own gifts.[1] Whether you are clergy or lay, a teacher, preacher, Sunday School teacher or a youth leader, or have other kinds of gifts, God can use you. Paul gives five characteristics of godly vessels, which we can apply to us as God's leaders.

First, we must be clean: a dirty vessel is no good. The godly person must first be sanctified by accepting Jesus and his salvation. Second, the vessel must be an instrument for special purposes. This means being available for the Lord to use. Are you available today? Moody was told that God wants a man fully sold out for him. Third, the vessel must be made holy. In other words, a Christian must be separated for God's ministry, like the vessels in the Temple. Fourth, a vessel must be useful to the Master. A broken vessel cannot hold wine. To be useful you must also be ready to train yourself for the job as God leads – and keep learning. Finally, a vessel must be prepared to do any good work. We cannot lay down conditions to God – we must be ready to go anywhere and do anything he wants. Paul told Timothy be ready to 'preach … in season and out of season'.[2] Are you ready? God showed this to me and I had to start preaching during my travels in India – so I carried a few sermons in the back of my Bible.

If you want to be a consecrated vessel for him and be of service to the Lord, you need all five characteristics.

Help us, Lord, to become consecrated vessels for you, useful and prepared to do any good work.

[1] 1 Cor 12 [2] 2 Tim 4:2

BIBLE IN A YEAR: **Jeremiah 19,20; John 8**

2 Timothy 3:1–9

Difficult Service

'... making the most of every opportunity, because the days are evil.'[1]

Paul's reference to the last days (v1) reveals his sense of urgency. The last days began after Jesus' resurrection and will continue to his second coming: we must make the most of the time God has given us.[2] In verses 2–4 we find a list of no fewer than eighteen vices that will characterise people in the last days. These conditions have always existed, but they will become more marked at the end. The warning is: don't give in to society's pressures, don't settle for comfort without commitment, but stand up against evil by living as God would have his people live.

In many parts of the world today this is easier said than done. If you have integrity, you will be condemned. When I worked in Philips India, in the Quality Control Department in the 1960s, I refused to pass a component which I knew was defective. My boss (under pressure from the top) tried to force me to do it, but I refused – so he passed it and I didn't get promotion for three years. God is no one's debtor, however. I bought a good camera and God opened for me a business to take photos at friends' weddings. In the end I was getting more money than if I had been promoted! Incidentally, the radios we made failed in the field because of that defect, and had to be recalled for repair.

In verses 6-9 Paul criticises the false teachers for their depraved living. We need to understand the Bible well. It's not enough just to learn without understanding and transformation. There is a need for proper theological teaching. We need to stand boldly for the truth.

May you become blameless and pure, children of God without fault in a depraved generation, shining like stars in the universe.[3]

[1] Eph 5:16 [2] Eph 5:16; Col 4:5 [3] Cf Phil 2:15

BIBLE IN A YEAR: **Jeremiah 21,22; Psalms 117,118**

Preparing for Christ

'Fix these words of mine in your hearts and minds ... Teach them to your children, talking about them when you sit at home'.[1]

Rather than being led astray by these false teachers, Timothy must continue in the teachings of which he had become convinced. Jewish children were customarily taught the Law at an early age and they had to commit parts of it to memory. The Holy Scriptures (our Old Testament) were able to prepare him – they disciplined him in obedience to God and pointed forward to the coming Messiah, through whom salvation by faith would become available. Timothy was a first-generation Christian.

A parent's work is vital. At home and at church we must realise that teaching small children is an opportunity and a responsibility. Paul says, 'Fathers, do not exasperate your children; instead, bring them up in the training and instruction of the Lord'.[2] Moses' words in Deuteronomy (quoted above) tell us to teach children at all times – not just in family prayers or Sunday School, but throughout the day. Small children can be taught to say 'Thank you, Jesus' before their meals; to pray for their classmates, friends and teachers who are sick, and so on. Children are quick to learn if we teach them.

The whole Bible is God's inspired Word: 'All Scripture is God-breathed' (v 16). The word used here is *theopneustos*, a combination of two other Greek words, *theos* (God) and *pneo* (breathe). This is one of the greatest texts in the New Testament. It means 'breathed out', in contrast with the breathing in of the breath of life when Adam was created.[3] Because it is inspired and trustworthy, it is our standard for testing everything and our source of guidance for how to live. We need to read it regularly and a Bible guide can help. I have been reading *Encounter with God* for over 50 years and have introduced many to it.

'The best book to read is the Bible. If you read it every day it will help you on your way, the best book to read is the Bible.'[4]

[1] Deut 11:18,19 [2] Eph 6:4 [3] Gen 2:7 [4] Anon, recorded by Colin Buchanan, 'The Best Book to Read'

BIBLE IN A YEAR: **Jeremiah 23,24; John 9**

Psalm 67

God's Glory and Power

May God be gracious to us and bless us and make his face shine upon us.[1]

This short psalm starts with a shout of praise and a petition for God's blessing, but it is also an evangelistic psalm, praying that the whole world would be filled with God's love. Every verse talks of God's relationship with the whole globe. Centuries later, Jesus would give the great commission, commanding that the gospel be taken to all nations.[2] Count yourself among that great crowd of believers worldwide who know the Saviour, praise him for his good news and share the gospel so that the harvest may be abundant.

We must also thank God for all who have preached the gospel to the nations. It is believed that the apostle Thomas came all the way to India in AD 52, to a people he did not know and to an area very strange to him, to preach the good news to my ancestors. He came to India before Paul went to the lands of the Roman Empire. Thomas had a much more difficult time.

He went to a different people and preached to them in a strange language, Tamil. God gave him the gift of tongues, as he never used a translator. God was with Thomas and blessed his ministry, as he obeyed his heavenly call. Everywhere he went he preached the gospel, planted a cross and built a church. Many temples whose priests had been converted became churches. Because of his ministry, the community of the Syrian Christians was established in Malabar or Kerala and I stand before you today because he converted my ancestors. There is a tradition in my family that we are descended from a Nambudri official of a local Rajah's court, who was converted by Thomas.

Pray for missionaries, especially Indian missionaries ministering in remote areas among tribal people, learning a new language and culture, translating the Bible and suffering many hardships.

Pray for all missionaries and praise God for their work.

[1] Num 6:24,25 [2] Matt 28:16–20

BIBLE IN A YEAR: **Jeremiah 25,26; John 10**

In and Out of Season

'We've a story to tell to the nations, that shall turn their hearts to the right'.[1]

In his closing message to Timothy, Paul stresses the importance of preaching the gospel so that the Christian faith would spread throughout the world. That is as important today as then and we should be ready to share the good news in our offices, schools, neighbourhoods and in the market place. This is by both words and deeds – so that, as Jesus said, people may 'see your good deeds and glorify your Father in heaven'.[2] Our honesty and integrity, our confidence in God at times of persecution and trouble, are a clear witness for Christ – and people ask questions. As Christian teams began to work in the Andhra floods in the 1970s, people asked, 'Why are you doing this?' And so the gospel could be preached.

Paul goes further and emphasises preaching at all times. If you examine verse 2 carefully you will note it is not only speaking of evangelism but of teaching to 'correct, rebuke and encourage … with … careful instruction'. This means we must always be ready to serve God in any situation, whether it is convenient or not. It is easy to spend time carefully preparing a sermon and delivering it from the pulpit, but unrehearsed preaching on the spot is very different. When I travelled around India on TAFTEE ministry I was often asked unexpectedly to preach, so I carried a few sermons in the back of my Bible. This was part of my covenant with God that I would never refuse a preaching invitation.

Paul's final testimony is here: 'For I am already being poured out as a drink offering' (v 6). This presents a picture of a drink offering poured on the lamb of sacrifice just before it was burned on the altar.[3] He is conscious that his fate is sealed for the sake of the gospel.

Lord, make us prepared to preach for you in season and out of season.

[1] H Ernest Nichol, 1862–1926 [2] Matt 5:16 [3] Num 28:1–8

BIBLE IN A YEAR: **Jeremiah 27,28; John 11**

2 Timothy 4:9–22

Forgiving those who Harm

'But if you do not forgive others their sins, your Father will not forgive your sins.'[1]

Paul was about to forsake this earth for the presence of his Lord. Though he has been deserted, Paul's love is revealed in verse 16: 'May it not be held against them'. He forgave his deserters for fearing to stand by him. Forgiveness is part of Christian ministry. Jesus forgave us from the cross, Stephen forgave his enemies, and now Paul forgives – but it is one of the hardest tasks.

As William Tyndale was being strangled and burned for translating the Bible into English, his last words were, 'Lord, open the eyes of the King of England'. Later, English Bibles were put into every church. Patrick Ireland was a survivor of the horrific Columbine High School massacre where 13 were killed and 24, including Patrick, were injured. Throughout his long recovery, Patrick learned that bitterness causes further wounding. God showed Patrick that the key to forgiveness was to stop focusing on what others had done to us and to focus on what God had done for us. Christ's words from the cross, 'Father, forgive them, for they do not know what they are doing',[2] revealed a purpose for Patrick; 20 years after the tragedy, he shared, 'Maybe I was chosen to forgive'.[3]

A nun was killed and thrown off a bus in India by a fundamentalist. The nun's sister visited the murderer in jail and said, 'We as a family forgive you'. With the help of the Bishop of Bhopal, they met the governor and requested him to commute the sentence. When the man was released they took him to their home in Kerala. He accepted Christ. The leader of the persecutors of Christians in the Khandamal massacres was witnessed to by the son of the man he killed; he became a believer and now preaches. Forgiveness is possible, though it needs the help of the Holy Spirit.

Lord, help us to forgive our enemies.

[1] Matt 6:15 [2] Luke 23:34 [3] Elsa Morgan, 'Chosen to Forgive', *Our Daily Bread*, Devotion, June 2, 2020

BIBLE IN A YEAR: **Jeremiah 29–31; Psalm 119:1–24**

JUDGEMENT AND RESTORATION

One of the things readers of the Old Testament prophets soon discover is the different kinds of writing these prophets use, often switching from one to another without giving notice. Jeremiah is an example of this. A quick look at almost any page will show that sometimes the text is set out as poetry and sometimes as prose narrative. Most of the poetry is what we call 'prophetic oracles' (or prophetic words), although in some of the poetry Jeremiah laments his own poor treatment from the people. The narratives tell of events in Jeremiah's life, as God instructs him to do certain things. There are also what we call 'prose sermons' – prophetic words of judgement or blessing, not in poetry but as prose.

The poetic prophetic words generally come in three types. Sometimes the prophets announce judgement against Israel, sometimes they announce judgement against the nations and sometimes they announce blessing for Israel. Since Jeremiah's ministry was after the fall of the northern kingdom of Israel, his words of judgement and blessing for Israel relate to the southern kingdom of Judah.

We find all these different kinds of writing in this part of Jeremiah, although judgement for Judah (eg 18:13–17) and blessing predominate. The announcements of blessing are especially prominent in chapters 30–33, sometimes called 'the Book of Consolation'. These chapters contain one of the high points of the Old Testament, Jeremiah's prophecy of the new covenant (31:31–34). This also illustrates one other thing: the New Testament writers interpret announcements of blessing for Israel with reference to Christ and the church.[1]

As we work with these chapters, be on the lookout for these different kinds of writing and the way they come together to contribute to the overall message of the book. That message is that God will judge his people and after the judgement of exile he will restore them, although the restoration will exceed anything Jeremiah ever imagined.

Phil Church

---

[1] For an example of this see Heb 8:7–12

Jeremiah 18,19

A Potter and a Pot

Start today with thanksgiving for the way God has guided your steps and made you the person you are today, a clay pot suitable for your work for God.

As the announcements in 18:1 and 21:1 show, Jeremiah 18–20 is a self-contained section. Within this, chapter 18 and chapters 19 and 20 are two parts marked by several parallels, the most obvious being the two reports about pots and potters. Each section contains a word of judgement, against Judah in chapter 18 and against an individual in chapter 20. In each section, Jeremiah laments the way he is treated. In today's reading there is also a play on the Hebrew word *ra'ah* (evil, disaster) which appears six times, sometimes referring to the evil people do and sometimes to the disaster that God will bring upon them.

First, God sends Jeremiah to a potter's workshop. He notices that if a pot doesn't turn out as expected the potter just starts again. There is still hope for Judah, who resembles a spoiled pot that God is about to judge. If the nation repents, God will relent and continue to reshape it. Jeremiah absorbed this lesson and announced it to the people. When the people rejected the warning (18:18), Jeremiah asked God to judge them. In the second pottery visit, Jeremiah buys a clay pot and takes it and the leaders of the people to a city gate where he announces God's judgement and smashes the pot, symbolising the disaster God would bring on the city. Jeremiah returned to the Temple precincts and announced that there was no longer any hope for Israel (19:14,15). Tomorrow we see the nation's response.

The song 'Have thine own way, Lord'[1] is probably based on these verses, although it emphasises the clay rather than the potter. In these chapters the Master Potter takes centre stage. They emphasise the Potter's forgiving grace when God's people repent, more than our willingness to be moulded by God.

We can take courage that God is always ready to forgive when we repent. We can confidently confess our wrongs, seeking God's forgiveness.

[1] Adelaide Addison Pollard, 1862–1934

BIBLE IN A YEAR: **Jeremiah 32,33; John 12**

Terror on Every Side

'Sing to the Lord! Praise the Lord! He rescues the oppressed from the power of evil people.'[1]

Here Jeremiah first speaks to Pashhur, the Temple security guard (vs 1–6); then he speaks to God (vs 7–12); and finally, he speaks to himself (vs 14–20). Yesterday we read of him in the Temple, announcing judgement on Jerusalem and Judah. In response, Pashhur had him beaten and imprisoned (v 2). On his release, he issued a devastating denouncement of Pashhur, giving the Lord's new name for him, 'Terror on Every Side' (v 3), and announced comprehensive judgement on him, all his friends and all of Judah.[2] Exile in Babylon was certain, as was death and burial in a foreign land for Pashhur and his friends.

Surprisingly, after this confident pronouncement, Jeremiah accuses God of deceiving him (vs 7–12). It is all very well to give Pashhur a new name, but what about when Jeremiah's foes hurl the same name at him (v 10)? He tried to keep silent but could not; his words just brought ridicule. However, this lament does not end on a negative note. As Jeremiah hears these taunts, he remembers that God is with him to deliver him and he commits his cause to God. Verses 14–20 reflect even deeper despair. Jeremiah curses the day he was born and the man who announced his birth, ending with the unanswered question, 'Why was I ever born?' (v 18, NLT).

Nevertheless, the chapter is not totally negative. Verse 13 separates the two laments, setting the context for both. Jeremiah calls on the believing community to sing praises to the Lord who rescues the needy from their enemies. God remains the same today. If we bring our despair to him, we may experience a new revelation of the character and activity of God, who understands our disappointment when our hopes don't eventuate.

Jeremiah's song of praise emerged from the depths of his despair. If we have the courage to be honest with God, like Jeremiah, we can find renewed confidence for living.

[1] Jer 20:13, GNB [2] The word 'all' appears eight times in verses 4–6

BIBLE IN A YEAR: **Jeremiah 34,35; John 13**

Jeremiah 21

God Against his People

'Praise the Lord, the God of Israel! He alone does these wonderful things. Praise his glorious name for ever! May his glory fill the whole world.'[1]

Jeremiah 21–24 represents a new block of material, in which God announces judgement against the kings of Judah for their injustice and against the false prophets for their lies. It is bracketed by two sections (21:1–10; 24:1–10), in which Jeremiah announces that God is bringing sword, famine and plague against them (21:9; 24:10). These paragraphs do not say why God is doing this, but it is clear that it is because of the injustice of the kings and the lies of the prophets.

The Babylonians have Jerusalem under siege and Zedekiah sends two messengers[2] to Jeremiah asking if God would act as he had in the past and cause the Babylonians to withdraw. This request reflects Israel's holy war traditions, where God fought on behalf of his people.[3] The response is only terrifying judgement.

The holy war traditions are turned upside down, with God coming against the king (vs 1–7), the people (vs 8,9) and the city (v 10). Surrender is the only way to escape with their lives.

The Lord addresses king, city and people in the prophetic word that follows (vs 11-14). The descendants of David are called back to faithfulness to the royal charter[4] or they will suffer God's anger. The city that relied on its geography for protection from enemy attack would be attacked by God and the people would be punished with fire kindled by the Lord for their evil deeds. These words are troubling, as we see God turning against his people. They do remind us, however, that we too need to take care with the way we live. For judgement always begins with the people of God.

They asked Jeremiah to ask the Lord to save his people. The troubling response was unrelenting judgement. God still calls his people to continual repentance today.

[1] Ps 72:18,19, GNB [2] This Pashhur is different from Jer 20:1 [3] Eg in the battle of Jericho (Josh 6) [4] Ps 72

BIBLE IN A YEAR: **Jeremiah 36,37; Psalm 119:25–48**

Three Wicked Kings

Lord, teach me to do what is right and to see that justice is done in my sphere of influence.

Two of God's covenants with Israel feature in this chapter. The Sinai covenant with its obligations on kings to do what is just and right[1] and the Davidic covenant promising that a descendant of his would always rule over Judah.[2] The Sinai covenant is implied in verse 3 and in verses 15 and 16 in the call to do what is just and right. It is explicit, too, in verse 9. The Davidic covenant is implied in verse 30. Judah's wicked kings thought the Davidic covenant had superseded the Sinai covenant, but the Ten Commandments, Judah's national constitution, encased in the Ark of the Covenant in the Temple alongside the king's palace, made it clear that it had not.

Josiah was a righteous king, but his three descendants, Shallum (aka Jehoahaz), Jehoiakim and Jehoiachin (aka Coniah) were not. Jehoiakim was probably king when God sent Jeremiah to go to the palace and announce God's judgement on it (v 1). Jeremiah called on the king to do what was right (v 3), announcing that if he did not, the palace would become a ruin. Verses 6 and 7 describe the destruction and verse 9 says why – 'Because they have forsaken the covenant of the LORD their God'.

The rest of the chapter announces judgement on these three wicked kings, climaxing with the solemn warning, 'none of his [Jehoiachin's] offspring will prosper, none will sit on the throne of David or rule any more in Judah' (v 30). Because of Jehoiachin's failure to obey the Sinai covenant, the Davidic covenant was also at an end. The followers of Jesus also have great and precious promises like the Davidic kings did, but these promises bring great responsibility. We are called to imitate Jesus in the way we live and to reflect his character.

Jesus is now seated at God's right hand, ruling the universe with God's power and authority. Worship Jesus your King today.

---

[1] Deut 17:18–20 [2] Ps 89:19–37

BIBLE IN A YEAR: **Jeremiah 38,39; John 14**

No God Like Our God

'Sing to God, sing in praise of his name, extol him ... Praise be to God!'[1]

Derek Kidner was probably on the right track when he suggested that Psalm 68 may have been composed for David's procession with the Ark of the Covenant to Jerusalem.[2] The opening words echo Moses' words when the ark moved.[3] God travelled through the wilderness (v 7) and came from Sinai in a procession to his sanctuary (vs 17,24–27). He now dwells in his sanctuary (v 35) as kings bring their tribute to the Jerusalem Temple (v 29).

While this general theme seems to fit, the details are complex and it is hard to see how the various stanzas fit together. One key to understanding is to notice the verbs describing God. Some tell what God has done (vs 7–10), some tell what God still does (vs 19,20) and some tell what God will do (vs 21,22). God is the God who acted in the past, who acts in the present and who will continue to act into the future.

High points of this psalm for me are verse 5, where God is described as a father to the fatherless and a defender of widows, two groups who are often the most vulnerable members of society, and verse 10 where God provides for the poor out of his rich bounty. Verse 19 is also a high point: our God is a burden-bearing God. The gods of the surrounding nations were lifeless gods who had to be carried, but our God is the God who daily carries our burdens. Since our God is like this, it is no wonder that the final stanza calls on the kings of the earth to sing praises to God and proclaim his power. There is no god like our God.

Select your own high point in Psalm 68 and meditate on it during the day. Bring your burdens to our burden-bearing God and leave them there.

[1] Ps 68:4,35 [2] Derek Kidner, *Psalms 1–72*, IVP, 1972, p256; 2 Sam 6:12–15 [3] Num 10:35

BIBLE IN A YEAR: **Jeremiah 40,41; John 15**

A Righteous King

Submit yourself to Jesus the King of kings and Lord of lords as you prepare your heart to hear from God today.

The judgement speeches against the wicked kings and false prophets in chapters 21–24 begin and end with Zedekiah,[1] although he is missing from chapter 22. In today's verses he is replaced by a new king with a name ('righteous Branch') that is a wordplay on his own name ('the Lord my Righteousness'), implying that he had not lived up to that name. There are two metaphors at work: the kings are pictured as shepherds of God's flock, something that endures today in our word 'pastor'; and the future ideal king is pictured as a shoot sprouting out of the stump of a dead tree.

These verses conclude the speeches of chapter 22 by announcing judgement on the kings who had caused God's people to be scattered (vs 1,2). Verses 3–8 announce a reversal of the exile in three sections. First, God announces the regathering of his people and the appointment of new shepherds to care for his flock; then God announces the 'righteous Branch', sprouting out of the dead stump of David's royal line. The section concludes by claiming that the significance of the Exodus from Egypt will be overshadowed by the significance of the return from exile.

Central to these verses is the announcement of the righteous Branch, 'The LORD Our Righteous Saviour' (v 6). Jeremiah anticipated a righteous king caring for and protecting God's people when they returned to their land from exile. From our New Testament perspective, we can identify the righteous Branch as Jesus the glorious king, ruling not just over the people of Judah but seated at God's right hand, ruling the universe with the power and authority of God.[2]

Whether we are in a formal pastoral role or not, the Bible asks us to act as shepherds and encouragers. Think of someone you can encourage today.

[1] Jer 21:1,3,7; 24:8 [2] Heb 1:1–4

BIBLE IN A YEAR: **Jeremiah 42,43; John 16**

Jeremiah 23:9–40

Fake News!

'May these words of my mouth and this meditation of my heart be pleasing in your sight, Lord, my Rock and my Redeemer.'[1]

In these days of internet and social media, fake news and alternative facts are common phenomena and it is frequently difficult to distinguish what is true from what is not. Where we get our information is important and we need to take care to check the sources and the evidence and to ask the right questions. We need to sift what we read and hear and use wisdom and insight to sort what is true from what is false.

This is not new. Fake news was rife in Jeremiah's time. According to this chapter, it was coming from false prophets who were leading the people away from God (vs 13,14). Jeremiah knew what questions needed to be asked if the people were to distinguish truth from falsehood. Had the prophets stood in the council of the Lord and had they been sent by the Lord? If they had, they would have spoken the Lord's words to his people and 'would have turned them from their evil ways and from their evil deeds' (vs 18–22). Because they had not stood there and because the Lord had not sent them, their words were false. Wrongdoing was rife.

God equips some in the church with the ability to speak a word from God into situations. God's people are called to discern whether what they say is valid. When it is, we can thank God and receive his word. God's people together are also called to speak prophetically into the societies where God has placed them. Whether we preach or prophesy in the church, or whether we spend our days in the wider society, we are all called to stand in the council of the Lord (v 22), listening for his voice and being ready faithfully to convey his message.

These false prophets were announcing peace and safety (v 17), when God's message was judgement (vs 19,20). How would you feel about bringing that word from God?

---

[1] Ps 19:14

BIBLE IN A YEAR: **Jeremiah 44–46; Psalm 119:49–72**

Two Kinds of Figs

Give thanks to our Lord Jesus Christ, who 'though he was rich, yet for your sake he became poor, so that you through his poverty might become rich.'[1]

In 597 BC, Nebuchadnezzar invaded Jerusalem and King Jehoiachin and most of the people were exiled to Babylon, leaving only the poorest of the land behind; and leaving Zedekiah as a puppet-king of Judah. Those who remained would have thought they were under God's favour, still in the land and still with access to the Temple for worship. They would have thought that the Babylonian exiles were under God's judgement, far away from God's presence. Ten years later, in 587, the Babylonians returned, destroyed the Temple, executed Zedekiah and exiled the remainder of the people. All of Judah was exiled away from their land.

Sometime in that ten-year period, Jeremiah had a vision of two baskets of figs placed in front of the Temple, perhaps first-fruits offerings.[2] One contained good figs and the other rotten figs. After a brief dialogue with Jeremiah, the Lord interpreted the vision in a way that was totally contrary to the thinking of the people. The good figs represented the exiles as the ones under God's favour. God would watch over them for their good, transform them and restore them to the land. God would be their God and they would be God's people. The rotten figs represented those who remained in the land. They would be afflicted with sword, plague and famine and ultimately exterminated.

The vision is not about the moral and spiritual qualities of either group, for all had been guilty of rebellion against God. It is about the grace of God, who reverses human values. This is the grace of God who chose a mixed multitude to be his people and of Jesus who chose sinners to be his friends.[3] This is the grace of God who entreats us with his unmerited favour.

Look back over your life and think about ways you have experienced God's unmerited favour. Spend some time giving thanks to God and look to the future with confidence.

---

[1] 2 Cor 8:9 [2] Deut 26:1-11 [3] Walter Brueggemann, *Jeremiah 1–25: To Pluck up and to Tear Down*, Eerdmans, 1988, p212

BIBLE IN A YEAR: **Jeremiah 47,48; John 17**

Jeremiah 25

The Lord Reigns

Ask God to hear the prayers of persecuted believers and to bring freedom and justice to people living under oppressive and unjust regimes.

I am writing in June 2021 with Covid-19 raging in many parts of the world. Over 180 million people have contracted the virus and almost two per cent of these have died. Yesterday saw another four hundred thousand new cases and over eight thousand deaths. I dare not suggest that God is using this pandemic to judge the world: I do not have such insights into the purposes of God. However, this chapter tells me that God is involved and God reigns, even during a pandemic. This chapter contains a variety of material, all of it reflecting God's sovereignty.

Jeremiah preached for almost a quarter of a century (v 3) and, as with all the other prophets God sent, few listened (vs 3,4,7). The outcome was the severe judgement of God through Nebuchadnezzar, with Judah becoming an 'everlasting ruin' (v 9). With the God who reigns, however, even 'everlasting' has its limits – seventy years (vs 11,12). Moreover, Nebuchadnezzar, who thought he was ruler of a great empire, is no more than God's servant (v 8), a king whose empire would also one day become desolate for ever (v 12). In verses 15–33 we learn that God's sovereignty extends to the other nations and, in verses 34–38, to the rulers of Judah. These too would be punished for their wickedness.

God is involved in the affairs of nations, then and now. I cannot foretell what the world will be like in 2022, but there will still be suffering and death, injustice, famine and war. It would be tempting to think that God is not involved. This chapter reminds us that God is always involved and that even so-called superpowers are subject to God. Their 'power is not the final reality'.[1]

'The idea that world events unfold without God being involved is even more frightening than the idea that he *is* involved.'[2] Let this idea inform your prayer.

[1] Walter Brueggemann, *Jeremiah 1–25, To Pluck up and to Tear Down*, Eerdmans, 1988, p219
[2] John Goldingay, *Jeremiah for Everyone*, Westminster John Knox, 2015, p130

BIBLE IN A YEAR: **Jeremiah 49,50; John 18**

Life and Worship

Loving God, give me a hearing ear, an understanding mind and a receptive heart to receive your word today and put it into action with my hands and feet.

Jeremiah 7:1–15 tells how God sent Jeremiah to stand at the gate of the Temple and proclaim to the gathering worshippers that unless they changed their ways they would encounter God's withering judgement: the destruction of the Temple in which they trusted and exile away from God's land. Those verses are essential background to this chapter – worth reading now.

Jeremiah 26 is a summary of what Jeremiah said in chapter 7; when he said it; and the response of the religious leaders and the people. They sentenced him to death. Jeremiah replied that he was speaking not his own words but God's and that these words from God represented an opportunity to repent (vs 12–15). They did repent, recalling how Micah had said similar things a century earlier[1] and that, at that time, Hezekiah had repented and God did not bring the judgement Micah

had prophesied. Jeremiah's life was spared, but an epilogue to the chapter (vs 20–23) relates the extradition and execution of Uriah, showing that speaking truth to power is always fraught with danger.

A glance at Jeremiah 7:8–11 brings into sharp focus what Jeremiah was standing against. The people, including their leaders, assumed that God was more interested in their worship than in their everyday lives. They thought God's Law was secondary to God's Temple. They also assumed that if God's messenger could be silenced the threat contained in his message could be nullified.[2] Neither assumption is true, not then and not now. On the other hand, if God's people heed God's words and repent, God has been known to change his mind about prophetic words of judgement.

Take the opportunity to examine your life to see if your words and actions from Monday to Saturday accord with your words of praise and worship on Sunday.

[1] Mic 3 [2] Walter Brueggemann, *Jeremiah 26–52: To Build and to Plant*, Eerdmans, 1991, p8

BIBLE IN A YEAR: **Jeremiah 51,52; Psalm 119:73–96**

Jeremiah 27

Don't Listen to Them!

'Jesus answered, "I am the way and the truth and the life. No one comes to the Father except through me."'[1] Exercise this privilege today.

Three times in this chapter Jeremiah tells his hearers not to listen to the false prophets. The events took place between Nebuchadnezzar's first invasion of Jerusalem, when he confiscated some of the implements of worship from the Temple (597 BC), and the siege when Temple and city were destroyed and the population exiled (587 BC). Holladay suggests the possibility of a rebellion against Nebuchadnezzar around 594 BC and dates the chapter then.[2] The false prophets were suggesting that those implements of worship would soon be returned and the exile would not happen (vs 9,14,16).

The Lord told Jeremiah to put a yoke on his neck to symbolise the yoke of Nebuchadnezzar[3] and advise the ambassadors of the surrounding nations, Zedekiah, and the priests and the people that the Lord, the Creator of all, gives authority to whomever he pleases. He had given authority and power to Nebuchadnezzar his servant. Judah and the surrounding nations would be subject to him until God handed his kingdom over to others and restored his people to their land.

We can read this chapter on two levels. The first level concerns the history of God's Old Testament people. When God had promised to give them the land, he also announced that rebellion would result in exile.[4] God was using Nebuchadnezzar to bring that about. This was a message that needed to be heard, and the false prophets had muted it. The other level is a reminder that God is involved in the affairs of the nations. He was then and he is now. The so-called superpowers are subject to God, who does what pleases him. That can give us courage in the face of a world that sometimes seems out of control.

Sometimes it is difficult to sift fake news from reality. Ask the one who claimed to be the 'truth' for discernment, to follow the true and ignore the false.

[1] John 14:6 [2] William L Holladay, *Jeremiah 2*, Fortress, 1989, p118 [3] See Jer 28 [4] Deut 28

BIBLE IN A YEAR: **Lamentations 1,2; John 19**

Save me, God, from my Foes

'I will praise God's name in song and glorify him with thanksgiving.'[1]

This psalm is an individual lament that seems to relate to the psalmist's concern for right worship in the Temple (v 9). Indeed, the disciples remembered verse 9 when Jesus cleared the Temple.[2] It may reflect circumstances like those we encountered on Friday in Jeremiah 26. Moreover, Jeremiah experienced something like verses 2 and 14.[3]

As you read the psalm, watch for 'I' statements, 'you' statements and 'they' statements. The psalmist brings his troubles to God in 'I' statements, mostly in verses 1–13, although they are mixed with 'you' statements, since the psalm is a prayer. 'You' statements are more prominent in verses 14–20, as he calls on God to rescue him. 'They' statements occur throughout the psalm, but are prominent in verses 22–28, where the psalmist asks God to condemn his enemies. The tone changes in verse 30, where the psalmist seems to recognise that God has heard his prayer and resolves to bring words of praise and thanksgiving. The last few verses may have been added later and probably refer to the return from exile in Babylon, applying God's answer to the psalm to all God's people.[4]

Two aspects of this psalm can be uncomfortable for Christians. First is the idea of lament itself. Lament doesn't sit well with us: we are much more comfortable bringing our praises to God. Psalm 69 reminds us that God also wants to hear about our pain. Verses 22–28 are more uncomfortable still. Here the psalmist asks God to judge his foes (unlike Jesus who asked his Father to forgive them). However, prayers like this also belong in the Bible. When we see atrocities against defenceless people, Psalm 69 gives us the warrant to pray for God's justice (not our own).

In the face of injustice, trust that God will deal justly with those who commit atrocities against others.

---

[1] Ps 69:30 [2] John 2:17 [3] See Jer 38:22 [4] Derek Kidner, *Psalms 1–72*, IVP, 1972, p268

BIBLE IN A YEAR: **Lamentations 3–5; John 20**

Jeremiah, Hananiah and God

Ask God, who by his Spirit inspired the Scriptures, to illumine your mind by the same Spirit and give you understanding as you read today.

In the Hebrew Bible the word for 'prophet' appears 16 times in this chapter, with about half applied to Hananiah and half to Jeremiah. Hananiah's name means 'the Lord is gracious' and his message seems to be that the Lord was more gracious than Jeremiah was suggesting.[1] Nevertheless, although he is clearly a false prophet, the text never says that explicitly. We must work it out. Jeremiah is wearing the yoke that God told him to wear[2] when Hananiah, who features only in this chapter, is abruptly introduced as 'the prophet' who announces in the Temple what the false prophets of 27:16 were saying: 'This is what the LORD Almighty, the God of Israel, says ... Within two years I will bring back to this place all the articles of the LORD's house' (vs 2,3). Jeremiah expresses his hope that what Hananiah was saying would happen. Then, to drive the message home, Hananiah breaks the yoke off Jeremiah's neck, announcing that God was about to break the yoke of Nebuchadnezzar. Jeremiah silently withdraws.

A short time later Jeremiah reappears with a word from God for Hananiah. 'The LORD has not sent you, yet you have persuaded this nation to trust in lies. Therefore ... This very year you are going to die' (vs 15,16). Two months later it happened. Verse 9 is right in the middle of the chapter. How do we sift false prophecy from true? Jeremiah points out that in the past the prophets had overwhelmingly announced disaster; Hananiah was announcing *shalom* (well-being). This new and different announcement needed to be put to the test. Sometimes when we are trying to sift what is false from what is true, we just need to wait and see, trusting God to work out his purposes.

In this world of conspiracy theories and fake news, ask God to give you discernment in your media consumption and to enlighten anyone you know who is consumed by conspiracies.

---

[1] Walter Brueggemann, *Jeremiah 26–52: To Build and to Plant*, Eerdmans, 1991, p23–24 [2] Jer 27:2

BIBLE IN A YEAR: **Ezekiel 1; John 21**

Living in Exile

'Open my eyes that I may see wonderful things in your law.'[1]

Walter Brueggemann writes that true prophecy 'is the capacity to say the right thing at the right time'.[2] This chapter is a great example. The conflict between true and false prophets that we have seen in chapters 27 and 28 continues, with several false prophets named and God's judgement on them pronounced. In contrast, we have Jeremiah's letter to the exiles (maybe 594 BC, near the start of the exile). Jeremiah was saying the right thing at the right time, but bringing what looked like strange advice and unwelcome news – followed by some welcome news.

The unwelcome news is that the Exile would last for 70 years (v 10). If human life is 70 years, then all those exiled to Babylon would die there. The strange advice was for them to make new lives in Babylon (vs 5–7), settling down, getting on with life, having children and seeking the well-being of Babylon. Their well-being was tied up with Babylon's well-being. The welcome news is in verses 11–14. While the exile would be long, it would not be permanent. The Lord had plans for good for his people, plans that involved prosperity and not harm (v 11). In due time he would restore them to Judah and restore fellowship with himself once more.

The apostle Peter uses the language of exile with the believers to whom he writes,[3] implying that the church (then and now) is in a similar position to Jeremiah's exilic audience. We are citizens of the age to come, living in the present evil age. Our temptation is to remain aloof and apart from the world; our calling is to live our Christian lives in the world, seeking its welfare.

Ask God for help to discover how to live as an exile where you do not really belong[4] and what it means to seek the well-being of your local community.

[1] Ps 119:18 [2] Walter Brueggemann, *Jeremiah 26–52: To Build and to Plant*, Eerdmans, 1991, p35
[3] 1 Pet 1:1; 2:11 [4] John 17:14–16

BIBLE IN A YEAR: **Ezekiel 2,3; Psalm 119:97–120**

Jeremiah 30

Back from Captivity

As you begin, submit yourself to God, asking him to speak into your life today through the Scriptures and to hear your prayers.

Jeremiah 30–33 is known as 'the Book of Consolation' since in these chapters Jeremiah elaborates on his prophecy of 29:14 that the exile would one day end and the Lord would bring his people back from captivity;[1] that is, he would 'give back to the covenant people the life, destiny, and well-being that belong to its identity as Yahweh's people'.[2]

Chapter 30 falls into three parts, each introduced by 'This is what the LORD says' (vs 5,12,18). Jeremiah begins by describing the horror of the time of Jacob's trouble and announcing that the Lord would bring this horror to an end in his time: 'do not be afraid … I am with you and will save you' (vs 10,11). The next section describes Israel's incurable wounds and ends with the promise that the Lord would cure these incurable wounds (vs 12–17). The third section describes the restoration and the rebuilding of Zion and the raising up of a new leader who would devote himself to the Lord (vs 18–22). Then, God announces, 'you will be my people, and I will be your God' (v 22).

The restoration of God's people at the end of exile saw only the partial fulfilment of these words. The key to their understanding is in verse 9 where this new leader is named 'David'. Of course, David was long dead. My Bible has a footnote for verse 9 directing me to Matt 1:1. The promised new ruler is Jesus, 'great David's greater Son' as the hymn 'Hail to the Lord's Anointed' calls him.[3] He is the one who 'came to break oppression and set the captive free, to take away transgression and rule in equity'. Ultimately, he is the one whom Jeremiah's prophecy anticipated.

As you pray today, think of suffering believers in many parts of the world. Ask God to strengthen their faith and hear their cries for deliverance.

---

[1] Jer 29:14; 30:3; 31:23 [2] Walter Brueggemann, *Jeremiah 26–52: To Build and to Plant*, Eerdmans, 1991, p47 [3] James Montgomery, 1771–1854

BIBLE IN A YEAR: **Ezekiel 4,5; James 1**

A New Covenant

Give thanks to God for his forgiveness and the blessings of the relationship you have with God in Christ.

This chapter is one of the high points of Jeremiah and of the entire Old Testament. Here God expresses his intention to bless 'all the families of Israel' (v 1) and restore them from Exile. It is striking in this chapter how certain expressions are repeated. Seven times we read, 'This is what the LORD says', fourteen times we read, 'declares the LORD' and there are eighteen 'I will' promises of restoration and blessing from the Lord for his people.

Two of these 'I will' promises are fundamental. The first is the covenant formula in verses 1 and 33: 'I will be their God and they will be my people'. This was the basis of God's relationship with his people, first declared in Exodus 6:7 and still there in Revelation 21:3. The other fundamental promise is in verses 31–34. When God exiled his people, the covenant relationship would have seemed to them to be over. They had broken the covenant

and God was judging them. Here, however, God promises to make a new covenant, unlike the former one. Two new covenant promises stand out to me. Under the old covenant God's laws were to be on their hearts.[1] That did not happen, but now God had a remedy. He himself would write the Law on their hearts and minds, enabling them to keep it. The other promise is that God would forgive their wickedness and resolve to remember their sins no more.

The New Testament applies the new covenant promises to Christ and the church. One example is in Jesus' words concerning the bread and wine at the Last Supper. As James Denney wrote over one hundred years ago, 'It is as though he had pointed to the prophecy in Jeremiah, and said, "This day is this Scripture fulfilled before your eyes".'[2]

Spend time meditating on some of the other 'I will' promises of Jeremiah 31 and apply them to your life.

---

[1] Deut 6:6 [2] James Denney, *The Death of Christ*, Hodder & Stoughton, 1902, p55

BIBLE IN A YEAR: **Ezekiel 6,7; James 2**

Jeremiah 32:1–15

Taking Risks for God

Faithful God, give me the grace to hear your call today and obey you.

God had promised his people that when they entered the Promised Land they would find cities and houses ready for them to inhabit, with vineyards and olive groves ready for them to eat the fruit.[1] Amos subsequently turned this promise on its head, announcing the time soon coming when they would no longer inhabit the houses they had built, nor would they drink the wine from the vineyards they had planted.[2] In this chapter, Jeremiah reverses Amos' prophecy of disaster: '[after the exile] houses, fields and vineyards will again be bought in this land' (v 15).

Jeremiah was imprisoned for announcing that the besieging army of Nebuchadnezzar would capture the city and that king and people would be exiled. There he heard a word from the Lord that one of his relatives was coming to sell him a piece of land. It happened – and Jeremiah, recognising that the Lord had spoken, bought the land and with careful attention to detail deposited the title deeds in a safe place.

Of course, nobody can take land away, it is always there, but as Amos had said, it can pass into the hands of others to enjoy its benefits. Jeremiah was so convinced that in time God would end the exile and restore the people to their land that he was ready to put his money where his mouth was and buy a piece of land,[3] believing God's promise that in time he would again enjoy the benefits of land ownership. It is one thing to say that we believe that God keeps his promises; it is quite another thing to take a risk like Jeremiah did by acting on those promises, even when, humanly speaking, the outlook looks bleak.

God calls us to take risks in faith. Can you take him at his word and trust him for the outcome, knowing that life is uncertain, but God is faithful?

[1] Deut 6:10–12 [2] Amos 5:10–12 [3] See John Goldingay, *Jeremiah for Everyone*, Westminster John Knox, 2015, p161–165

BIBLE IN A YEAR: **Ezekiel 8,9; Psalm 119:121–144**

Jeremiah 32:16-44

Nothing too Hard for God?

Sovereign Lord, for whom nothing is too hard, strengthen my feeble faith today.

Yesterday we reflected on Jeremiah's faith, which enabled him to risk buying a field even though he was convinced that the Babylonians were about to empty the land of its inhabitants. Today we discover the source of Jeremiah's faith. When God announced to Abraham and Sarah that they would have a child, he said to Abraham, 'Is anything too hard for the LORD?'[1] Jeremiah answers this question in verse 17: 'Nothing is too hard for you.' Then God asks it again in verse 27. Jeremiah's prayer (vs 17–25) and God's response (vs 26–44) both rehearse this idea.

In his prayer, Jeremiah looks back and lists the 'too hard' things God had done in Israel's past, including creating earth and heaven, redeeming his people in the Exodus and giving them their land. Then he looks out at the siege ramps and remembers God's instruction to buy the field. God responds to Jeremiah's prayer by telling of the 'too hard' things he was about to do. First, he was about to give Jerusalem (which God loves)[2] into the hands of the Babylonians who would destroy it. Then, God was going to restore Israel to the land so that they would live in safety, so that once again fields would be bought and sold throughout Judah and Benjamin (where Jeremiah's field was).

There is a more sombre aspect to God's answer – the catalogue of Israel's rebellion (vs 30–35). God's response to that is another too-hard thing that God was about to do. God would make an everlasting covenant with his people and give them singleness of heart, enabling them to fear God and never turn away again. This he has done in Jesus.

Are there any too-hard things in your basket? Retrieve them today and commit them to God, who loves to do what is too hard.

[1] Gen 18:14   [2] Ps 78:68

BIBLE IN A YEAR: **Ezekiel 10,11; James 3**

Psalm 70

Hurry up, God!

Lord, you are my help and my deliverer. May I experience your saving help this day.

This short psalm, which also appears as the last five verses of Psalm 40, begins and ends by asking God to hurry up and answer the psalmist's prayer. Nobody knows whether it first existed here and was later combined with a psalm that begins, 'I waited patiently for the LORD', or whether it was there in the first place and was deemed important enough to exist on its own. Whatever the case, it reminds us that while it is necessary to wait patiently for God to answer our prayers, it is sometimes appropriate to ask God to hurry up. Maybe it is doubly appropriate here, because this plea appears twice in Ps 40 (vs 13,17) and twice in Ps 70 (vs 1,5).[1]

Apart from two lines in verse 5, this psalm only contains prayers. Those two lines are the basis for the prayers: 'I am poor and needy ... You are my help and my deliverer'. When we are conscious of our need and of God's ability to meet that need, then we can pray in faith. In between the pleas for God to hurry up is the five times repeated expression 'may those ...'. The first three requests are for God to shame the psalmist's enemies. The last two requests concern all who seek God and long for him to act: may God bring them joy and gladness, and may he open their mouths with the confession 'The LORD is great!' (v 4).

Is this climax to these five petitions the ultimate outcome of our answered prayers? As we look at our need and God's ability to meet that need, and as we experience God's grace in doing so, we too should give thanks and praise to God, declaring his greatness.

God may answer our prayers with 'Yes', 'No', or 'Wait'. Would this psalmist be satisfied with 'No' or 'Wait'? Should we? Be encouraged and continue to pray.

[1] It also appears in Pss 22:19; 38:22; 71:12; 141:1

BIBLE IN A YEAR: **Ezekiel 12,13; James 4**

Super-Fulfilment

'... his compassions never fail. They are new every morning; great is your faithfulness.'[1]

This last chapter of Jeremiah's 'Book of Consolation' contains seven promises of restoration. Verses 1–5 set the context during the destruction of Jerusalem and verses 6–26 announce the restoration. The first promise contains several 'I will' statements as the Lord promises to bring health and healing, peace and security, and cleansing and forgiveness. The remaining promises are all introduced with statements indicating that the Lord is speaking.

There will be the sounds of joy and gladness and wedding songs. Songs of praise will be once again heard in the Temple. Ruined cities will again be inhabited and there will be pastures for the shepherds and their flocks. There will be a new king, 'a righteous Branch' (v 15) sprouting from the line of David. David's enduring dynasty is reaffirmed and finally, in the last two promises, God affirms that the order of creation, with day following night, indicates that there will always be a king seated on David's throne and Levitical priests ministering before God. God's people will be as countless as stars in the sky and as measurless as the sand on the beach. 'For I will restore their fortunes and have compassion on them' (v 26).

We might question whether the promises about a king and priests have been fulfilled, but when we look back with New Testament hindsight we learn that Jesus is 'great David's greater son'.[2] Jesus the king from the line of David is seated for ever at God's right hand. The book of Hebrews modifies the promise about an enduring Levitical priesthood by claiming that Jesus, the new priest like Melchizedek, is ministering in the presence of God, interceding for us.[3] He brings to completion all that the descendants of Levi anticipated.

God planned that Israel would be a kingdom of priests and a holy nation. This plan now includes kings and priests drawn from every nation. A true 'super-fulfilment'.[4]

---

[1] Lam 3:22,23 [2] James Montgomery, 'Hail to the Lord's Anointed' [3] Heb 6:20; 7:25
[4] John Goldingay, *Jeremiah for Everyone*, Westminster John Knox, 2015, p172

BIBLE IN A YEAR: **Ezekiel 14,15; James 5**

Jeremiah 34

Making Promises to God

'Speak, LORD, for your servant is listening.'[1] Teach me to obey your word to me.

Two things from Israel's history can clarify this chapter. First, the legislation for a sabbatical year.[2] The Law recognised that people who had fallen into debt could deal with their debts by committing to work for a neighbour until they were extinguished. The sabbatical year, which Israel had agreed to when they entered a covenant with God, provided for the release of these debt slaves every seven years, with any remaining debt cancelled. Second, a covenant ceremony sometimes involved the parties to the covenant bisecting an animal and walking between the pieces, agreeing to be similarly bisected if they broke the covenant.[3]

Although the people of Judah had not been in the habit of freeing their debt slaves, a time did come when king Zedekiah and the people made a covenant to do so (v 8), probably sealing the covenant by bisecting a calf (vs 18,19). They freed their slaves, but afterwards changed their minds and

enslaved them again. God had something to say about that. In 588 BC Nebuchadnezzar had temporarily withdrawn from his siege of Jerusalem. God announced that he was about to bring him back (v 22). Moreover, in a characteristic play on words, Jeremiah announced that because they had not released their slaves, God was going to release them – to the sword, plague and famine. Jerusalem and Judah would face certain destruction.

Nebuchadnezzar's siege might have been the reason why the people freed their slaves. 'Perhaps God will see our faithfulness and save us', they may have said. Nebuchadnezzar's withdrawal may have caused them to change their minds and take back their slaves. I speculate, of course. But, which one of us has not made promises to God when things are bad, only to renege on those promises when things improve?

Ask God to search your heart to see if there are commitments you have made that you have not kept. Can you commit to keep them?

---

[1] 1 Sam 3:9,10 [2] Deut 15:1–18 [3] See the example in Gen 15:7–21

BIBLE IN A YEAR: **Ezekiel 16,17; Psalm 119:145–176**

Scripture Union

Helping you share the **good news** this *Christmas*

ONLY £10 FOR A PACK OF 10

A story of old, but still here t[...]
It's changed who I am in eve[...]
It's awesome, fantastic, amazing[...]
And that's why I'm here - tellin[...]

God Became Like Me? features stunning line illustrations for children to colour in while reflecting on a poetic retelling of the real Christmas story.

Available in packs of ten, these beautiful little books are ideal for sharing the good news of Jesus' birth with children in your community.

Get yours at su.org.uk/godbecamelikeme

BETWEEN THE TESTAMENTS

'...you have turned from the way and by your teaching have caused many to stumble ...

You have wearied the LORD ... By saying, "All who do evil are good in the eyes of the LORD, and he is pleased with them" ... Return to me, and I will return to you'.[1]

With warnings such as these, the Old Testament ends and the voice of prophecy falls silent. We turn the page and read: 'This is the genealogy of Jesus the Messiah the son of David, the son of Abraham'.[2] In turning that page we have leapt over more than four hundred years, when the voice of God was apparently silent. In fact, however, a great deal happened during that time which challenged and shaped the Jewish people.

Earlier in their history, successive generations had endured oppression under the pharaohs in Egypt (about 1700–1300 BC). Later, in 721 BC, the northern kingdom of Israel was conquered by Assyria (northern Iraq today) and most of its people were deported to Assyrian territory. In 587 BC the smaller kingdom of Judah fell to Nebuchadnezzar of Babylon.[3]

Psalm 137 catches the exiles' mood: 'How can we sing the songs of the LORD while in a foreign land?'[4] It is likely, however, that during this period of exile, when Jews were denied the usual cycle of festivals and worship at the Jerusalem Temple, the synagogue emerged as an alternative way to worship.

Other tragic upheavals were to follow. In 539 BC King Cyrus of Persia – who had already conquered the neighbouring Medes to create the Medo-Persian Empire – defeated Babylonian forces and gained control of an empire that stretched from the Persian Gulf in the east to the Mediterranean coast of Turkey. Isaiah calls Cyrus God's 'anointed' and 'my shepherd' because his policy was to allow the Jewish exiles to return to their own land.[5] Judah became one of the many provinces of his empire.

In 458 BC Ezra was permitted to return to Jerusalem, carrying with him 'the Book of the Law of Moses' (Genesis–Deuteronomy),[6] probably in a form very close to the text familiar to us. Later, in 445, Nehemiah arrived to rebuild the walls.[7]

The Jewish people then experienced a century of relative stability – until

---

[1] Mal 2:8,17; 3:7, italics added [2] Matt 1:1 [3] 2 Kings 25 [4] Ps 137:4 [5] Isa 44:28; 45:1,13 [6] Neh 8:1 [7] Neh 2

another brilliant general threw the world into turmoil once more. Alexander the Great of Macedon (northern Greece), with an army of forty thousand, defeated the Persian army (a hundred thousand strong) at the battle of Issus in south-eastern Turkey in 333 BC. Jewish people became part of Alexander's empire, which stretched from Greece to the borders of India in the east and to Egypt in the south. After his early death in 323, his empire was divided among his Macedonian successors – the Seleucids in Syria and the Ptolemies in Egypt. Greek became the dominant language.

The new regime was not so bad for a while – until the Seleucid Antiochus IV became king (175–164 BC). He styled himself 'Epiphanes' – 'God manifest', though his opponents preferred to call him 'Epimanes' – 'Madman'. Ruling from Syria, he persecuted Jews by forbidding circumcision and Sabbath-keeping. In the Temple he built an altar to the Greek god Zeus. Resistance arose under the leadership of Judas (known as Maccabeus, 'The Hammer'), a member of a priestly family. After seven years (167–160 BC) their guerrilla tactics succeeded in defeating the Seleucid army. The Temple, which had been defiled by the Seleucids, was rededicated and its regular rituals and festivals restored. The restoration continues to be celebrated at the annual festival of *Hanukkah*.

For those of us who live in stable democracies, it is hard to imagine how the Jews were affected by this sequence of terror, conquest and exile, interrupted by calmer periods. Perhaps we need to think more often about countries today where people suffer comparable danger and upheaval. The website en.wikipedia. com on 'Ongoing armed conflicts' maintains a disturbingly long list of ongoing conflicts around the world. If we live in the West we can hardly begin to imagine the level of fear, the loss of life and livelihood and the number of refugees associated with such events. The situation can inform our prayers, however, and help us to understand why families will cross deserts and face dangerous seas in the hope of finding asylum.

So how *did* the Israelites cope? They knew how to *lament*, and they had resources for that in their scriptures. Two-thirds of the psalms are laments, in which they could pour out their anxieties and find hope in the compassion of God. They could appeal to promises of God, such as: 'Comfort, comfort my people, says your God. Speak tenderly to Jerusalem, and proclaim to her that her hard service has been completed ... A voice of one calling: "In the wilderness prepare the way for the LORD".[8]

Some of them wrote *stories*, including tales of miraculous deliverance from the hands of tyrants, designed to boost morale and trust in God's providence.

And of course they had scriptures to reflect on, even though the Old Testament as we know it was not yet complete. Imagine them listening to these words from Exodus:

'I have indeed seen the misery of my people in Egypt. I have heard them crying out because of their slave drivers, and I am concerned about their suffering. So I have come down to rescue them from the hand of the Egyptians'.[9]

Hearing that, they might reflect: God *is* with us, he knows our sufferings and he wants to set us free. Maybe not by a miraculous escape right now, but we know that God has not forgotten us. Surely he *will* deliver us...

Some who lived during that period of upheaval were writing what would become recognised as scripture. Though

Malachi is the last book in our Old Testament, sections of some books – parts of Psalms and Proverbs, Ecclesiastes, Chronicles and Daniel – were probably written later.

Other books were written during the four centuries before the birth of Christ, books expressing faith and hope in the midst of tragedy. Fourteen of these books form the *Apocrypha*. These, according to Martin Luther, 'are not considered equal to the Holy Scriptures, but are useful and good to read.' Here is a brief description of some of them:

- *1 Esdras* – a rewriting (during the first century AD?) of biblical history from the time of King Josiah to the reforms of Ezra. (Esdras is the Greek version of the Jewish name Ezra.)

- *Ecclesiasticus* (or 'The Wisdom of Jesus son of Sirach') – a collection of wise sayings and proverbs. It ends with a thankful celebration of God's goodness and an appeal to readers to seek wisdom. Written about 180 BC.

- *Wisdom of Solomon* – another celebration of the importance of wisdom to guide our lives. Written about 50 BC.

[8] Isa 40:1-5 [9] Exod 3:7,8

- *Tobit* – the story of a faithful Jew, now an exile in Nineveh. He goes blind, but because of his faithfulness his sight is later restored by an angel. Written about 200 BC.

- *Judith* – The story of a Jewish woman living in Jerusalem at the time when it was besieged by the Assyrians. She sneaks into the enemy's camp at night and cuts off the head of the Assyrian general – at which the whole army takes fright and flees. It's an unlikely story, with many historical inaccuracies, but great for boosting the morale of Jews facing danger in later times. Written about 100 BC.

- *1 and 2 Maccabees* – These books record the triumph of Jewish resistance fighters in the face of persecution by the Seleucid ruler Antiochus IV Epiphanes in the period 167–160 BC. The festival of *Hanukkah* celebrates the rededication of the Temple after the Maccabean victory. Written between 150 and 120 BC.

The full text of these books can be read online (Authorised Version) at sacred-texts.com or (in modern English) in some editions of the New Revised Standard Version.

We return, finally, to the ongoing story of the Jewish people. The Maccabees established the Hasmonean dynasty, and again for a while the Jews lived at peace in their own land. It was not to last. Since 510 BC the Romans had gradually been building an empire which, by the middle of the first century BC, embraced nearly all the lands surrounding the Mediterranean Sea. In 63 BC the Roman general Pompey successfully besieged Jerusalem and brought it under Roman control. The extent of this control is made abundantly clear in the New Testament. In 37 BC the Romans installed Herod – a high-ranking Arab from Idumea, a desert territory south of the Dead Sea – as 'king of the Jews'. He died in 4 BC. If you wonder how he could die in 4 BC and still appear in the story of Jesus' birth, the answer lies in a small miscalculation by the sixth-century monk Dionysius Exiguus ('Dennis the Little'), who created our *Anno Domini* dating.

Now we have reached the beginning of a new era, when the silence of those four hundred years since the time of Malachi is broken by the coming of 'the Word made flesh'.[10]

[10] See John 1:14

Luke 9:51 – 13:35

DISCIPLESHIP IS HARD AND COSTLY

With the words 'As the time approached' (9:51), Luke begins a new section in his Gospel. It should have marked the start of a new chapter. Robert Estienne,[1] who created our verse numbers, did so while travelling, so he sometimes missed the spot. Stephen Langton[2] had much earlier invented reasonable chapter divisions, but he failed to discern this important dividing line.

Jesus recognises that his 'time' is near, the time of his suffering and execution. Expecting pain and death, Jesus 'set his face' (9:51, AV) towards Jerusalem. Luke took ten chapters to get Jesus through Samaria to Jerusalem and his roadmap is sometimes vague – 'a village of the Samaritans', 'a certain village', 'one town and village after another'.

Nevertheless, the decisive moment had come. Jesus was on his journey to his cross – but he was in no hurry to get there. He could linger. He worried about his disciples. He had much to teach them. He wanted to warn them of what lay ahead, to explain the cost of discipleship, to compose and narrate the sterner parables of death and judgement. He needed to give the disciples a practice lesson, sending them out into the world to learn how to tread the hard road of discipleship without his presence. How long did that take? It could have taken months, even a year, for Jesus and his retinue to reach Jerusalem. Some suggest that Luke compiled the teaching in this section from other gospels or elsewhere in Jesus' ministry. But the purpose of a Gospel is not to provide an exhaustive chronological record of Jesus' life but to teach us who Jesus was and what he said. Let us, then, begin Luke's long narrative of the journey from Galilee to Jerusalem. Like the disciples of old, we need to heed the warnings and understand the risks. We too need to know the cost.

John Harris

FOR FURTHER READING

R Alan Culpepper, *The Gospel of Luke: The New Interpreter's Bible*, Abingdon, 1995

---

[1] Robert Estienne, French printer, 1501–59 [2] Stephen Langton, Archbishop of Canterbury, 1150–1228

Stepping Over the Border

'God be in my head, and in my understanding; ... God be in my heart, and in my thinking.'[1]

'As the time approached' (v 51) marks a watershed in Luke's Gospel, beginning a darker period in Jesus' life. We leave behind the Jesus of stilling the storm and feeding the five thousand. We leave the glorified Jesus of the mount of transfiguration, to commence a more sombre journey with Jesus, focused on the path to his cross. They are now a larger group of women and men than just the 12 disciples.[2] In today's reading, Jesus and his companions cross a geographical and psychological border, leaving the familiarity of Galilee to enter a less comfortable, more alien environment.

Across the border, they encounter their first challenge. A village refuses to lodge them overnight – an important real-life lesson for the disciples at the beginning of a journey when Jesus will say much about rejection. We must not condemn the poor Samaritans. They too are under Roman rule and, suddenly, a large band of people turns up from rebellious Galilee, well known for breeding revolutionaries. They fear provoking the ruthless vengeance of the Romans. Yet James and John's vengeance would have been even worse – the destruction of the village. They have much still to learn about what discipleship means.

Along the journey, some are drawn to Jesus. The one who pledges to follow Jesus anywhere did not know that the path led to the cross. It is possible that he did follow and later faced death in the persecution of the first Christians. Jesus' words to the other two seem harsh, but we lack the details of the whole conversation. Both excuses amount to the same spiritual dilemma: 'I'll be free after my father dies'; 'I need to sort out my family's affairs first'. These are hard lessons for us all. Discipleship is unconditional. It may lead to suffering, even to a cross.

Lord of the hard road, help us to step out of our comfort zone, to cross the difficult borders and to tread where you have trod.

[1] Sarum prayer c1400 [2] Luke 8:1–3

BIBLE IN A YEAR: **Ezekiel 18,19; 1 Peter 1**

We are *all* on a Mission

'May I run the race before me, / strong and brave to face the foe, / looking only unto Jesus / as I onward go.' [1]

Jesus' followers keep increasing in number. He commissions not just the 12 but 72 more disciples! And he sends them all. From Luke's account, they are being sent into Samaria, for reasons explained in Jesus' outburst. Very few Jews in Galilee had recognised the Messiah foretold by their own prophets – not Bethsaida where he fed the five thousand; not Capernaum where the disabled man was let down through the roof. We can learn much from Jesus' instructions. Churches like mine seem to have abandoned the practice of sending out members door to door. Are we in danger of forsaking our mission entirely? Does financial support for mission and church organisations relieve us of personal responsibility?

What does Jesus say? Well, 12 crucial things.[2] 'The harvest is plentiful' (the world needs the church's mission). '... the workers are few' (there is more work than labourers). 'Ask the Lord of the harvest' (prayer does matter). 'Go!' (all are sent, not just high-profile people). '... like lambs among wolves' (God's mission is vulnerable; the forces of evil are real). '...do not greet anyone on the road' (we need to be single-minded). '...say "Peace to this house"' (be a peacemaker). 'Stay there, eating and drinking whatever they give you' (be gracious; accept the hospitality offered, particularly by culturally different people). '...tell them, "The kingdom of God has come near"' (be transparent about your motives). '...when ... you are not welcomed' (we won't always succeed). '... say, "Even the dust from your town we wipe from our feet"' (put failure behind you and keep trying). '...the kingdom of God has come near' (we are not alone; God is always near). Jesus' principles guide us in every generation. The context, means and forms of mission will change, but its basis in God's redemptive love remains constant.

Lord of the church's mission, teach us again how to be your witnesses, send us out once more into your world, feeling your constant presence on the road.

---

[1] Katie Wilkinson, 1859–1928, 'May the mind of Christ' [2] R Alan Culpepper, *The Gospel of Luke: The New Interpreter's Bible*, Abingdon, 1995, p222

BIBLE IN A YEAR: **Ezekiel 20,21; 1 Peter 2**

Pride or Humility?

"'Take up your cross", the Saviour said, / "if you would my disciple be. / Take up your cross ... and humbly follow after me."'[1]

The disciples returned, jubilant about their achievements. Jesus had taken a risk, sending *everybody* out, not just the twelve. Now they return, full of tales of their power over evil spirits. Jesus' response is elation (v 21). Evil has retreated a little before his disciples. This is prophetic! Victory over the forces of evil still awaits the cross and the final vanquishing of evil at the end of time, but Jesus senses the beginning of the end. Those who go in his name need not fear 'snakes and scorpions' (v 19), the deadly poison of evil which cannot overcome us. Neither the disciples nor we are physically safe from accident or disease in this life. Many of Jesus' followers would go on to die a martyr's death – but death has no sting.[2] We are safe, not from earthly suffering, but safe for eternity. In Jesus' final prayer for his disciples, he explicitly says that he does not ask for their immunity from suffering, but that 'you protect them from the evil one'.[3]

Jesus' other reaction to the disciples' excitement is a stern warning not to take pride in their successes as if they were personal achievements. All spiritual abilities are given to us, not earned. They all come from God. No one should feel personal pride in gifts like preaching or healing or leadership. None are deserved. All are bestowed. It is sad to see Christian organisations advertising their 'signs and wonders' and adopting personal names such as 'X X Ministries'. We see far too often the adulation of prominent Christian leaders and their own easy acceptance of their fame. All that ultimately matters is that our names are written in God's eternity. We have nothing spiritual to take pride in. We were bought at great cost. We belong to God, who says, 'I have engraved you on the palms of my hands'.[4]

Lord of your church, gladly we take your spiritual gifts with outstretched hands. Forgive our pride. Thank you that our names are written in heaven.

[1] Charles Everest, 1814–1877 [2] See 1 Cor 15:55 [3] John 17:15 [4] Isa 49:16

BIBLE IN A YEAR: **Ezekiel 22,23; Psalms 120–122**

Ignoring False Boundaries

'[Grant] us in this world knowledge of your truth, and in the world to come, life everlasting.'[1]

Jews made no distinction between religious and civil law. The lawyer, an expert in the Mosaic Law, knew the Torah – but it is not easy to find eternal life clearly affirmed there. The lawyer was challenging Jesus. He posed the question of the ages, asked by all societies and cultures down through time. How do we find the afterlife? Can we live for ever? Eternity belongs to God and so Jesus asked him what God's Law said. In the spirit of the old covenant, the lawyer answered well: loving God and loving our neighbour.

The lawyer, however, annoyed that Jesus turned the question back on him, went a step further, trying to trick Jesus. First-century Judaism was obsessed with boundaries, with detailed regulations about relationships between Jews and Gentiles, Jews and Samaritans, men and women, and so on. Protecting these boundaries masqueraded as a religious duty. Within all these strictures, who is my neighbour?

So Jesus tells the 'good Samaritan' story and asks the question on which the lawyer had hoped to impale Jesus. Which traveller was the neighbour? The lawyer cannot even bring himself to say 'the Samaritan', but his circuitous answer says more than he intended. Jesus shifts the question from the boundaries of legislated social interaction to the essential nature of neighbourliness with a story that shatters the human boundaries of class and ethnicity. The duty of neighbourliness reflects the love of God and of others. Mercy sees only need and responds with compassion. Those who show mercy show that they belong to the kingdom, because they exhibit the behaviours of the age to come, the qualities which are the mark of those on the path to eternal life.

Lord of the age to come, give us the grace to be people of compassion, people of true mercy, fit for eternal life.

[1] Chrysostom, 347–407

BIBLE IN A YEAR: **Ezekiel 24,25; 1 Peter 3**

'God be at Mine End'[1]

'I fear no foe, with thee at hand to bless … Where is death's sting? Where, grave, your victory? / I triumph still, if thou abide with me.'[2]

I am so glad it fell to me to share this psalm with you. I relate so deeply to it. Like the psalmist, I knew God as a child, knowing and loving my parents' Jesus long before my earliest memories. Then I, too, have become 'old and grey' (v 18) and want to feel God's presence closer to me as my physical and mental strengths wane. The psalmist's enemies were flesh and blood. He knew that only God had enabled him to defeat them. Now he grows old, his enemies remain but he knows his increasing weakness. He needs God more than ever. For most of us, the enemies which attack us are spiritual but no less dangerous. Evil forces can mislead us, grasp us and entrap us.

It has been a privilege to follow Jesus for 80 years, but it has given the forces of evil many opportunities to assail me. With the psalmist, I can only feel that it has always been God who rescued me and brought me through, time and again, to a spiritually safe place. I don't want to become like some of my friends who are losing their memories but, if I do, God will not forget me. Deep down, I know that Jesus has opened the path to eternal life. That is my destiny. The psalmist had no such assurance. He could only reach out in blind faith that, even from the grave, God could raise him to life (v 20). He could only stretch out the trembling fingers of his Old Testament mind to try to touch what we can know with certainty: 'God has given us eternal life, and this life is in his Son.'[3] That is the only true peace that can fill my heart and mind, even as little of life remains.

Lord of my destiny, thank you that you are ever with me. Help me to trust you, in light and darkness, knowing that my eternal future is safe with you.

[1] Sarum Prayer, *Horae Beatae Mariae Virginis*, 1514 [2] Henry Lyte, 1793–1847, 'Abide with me' [3] 1 John 5:11

BIBLE IN A YEAR: **Ezekiel 26,27; 1 Peter 4**

Luke 10:38–42

A Tale of Two Women

'Forth in your name, O Lord, I go, / my daily labour to pursue, / you, Lord, alone resolved to know / in all I think, or speak, or do.'[1]

This simple story is often explained too simplistically. It is not about hospitality, the Holy Spirit's gift,[2] which Jesus regularly enjoyed. In Luke's Gospel, this story of a woman determined to hear Jesus follows that of a male lawyer who only wanted to hear himself. Jesus knew this little household, although Lazarus seems absent. The women invited him in. Martha went to prepare the meal while Mary sat at Jesus' feet, the traditional pose in front of a rabbi, assuming the position of a male disciple. This annoyed Martha, who was probably more upset about Mary's posture than her help in preparing the meal, thinking that Mary was being overfamiliar. Her criticism is not addressed to Mary but to Jesus – who, she asserts, should have said something about it. Her outburst contains four first-person pronouns (my, me, myself, me) as if she is affronted, even jealous. Jesus, however, accepted Mary's role, thus inviting all women to be disciples. His response to Martha was far deeper than mere housework. Martha was letting herself get distracted and anxious. Her mental state was hampering her spiritual life.

Here were two very different women, whose spirituality would always be different, but who would love and follow Jesus in their own ways. On another day, Mary will anoint Jesus with perfumed oil and wipe his feet with her hair, an act which Jesus declared was preparing his body for death.[3] Martha, always the practical one, met Jesus when he came to raise Lazarus while Mary stayed inside, mourning. John recorded Martha's conversation with Jesus, which prompted one of his most important sayings, 'I am the resurrection and the life'; Martha responded, as we all must: 'I believe that you are the Messiah, the Son of God'.[4]

Lord of our days, help us not to be distracted from you by the busyness of life, nor to let our anxieties muffle your voice in our hearts and minds.

[1] Charles Wesley, 1707–88, altered [2] 1 Pet 4:9–11 [3] John 12:1–8 [4] John 11:25–27

BIBLE IN A YEAR: **Ezekiel 28,29; 1 Peter 5**

Luke 11:1–4

Release us from our Sins

'Almighty ... God, who hatest nothing that thou hast made, and dost forgive the sins of all them that are penitent: Create and make in us new and contrite hearts'.[1]

Here is Luke's shorter version of this greatly loved, deeply meaningful but dangerous prayer. I have often participated in translating it into Indigenous Australian and Pacific languages. Praise God, most language groups have a Christian community today. Foreign translators no longer see themselves translating the Bible for unbelievers but supporting local Christians doing it for themselves. We usually begin with a Gospel, but so often people ask for the Lord's Prayer first, wanting to express all the depth of its meaning in the language of their hearts.

'Father' is a simple word in all languages, often a baby word. We can draw close to God, even call him 'Father', an intimacy that is ours even though God's name is a holy name, which he alone can possess. 'Hallowed' challenged us in languages lacking a word for God's good and perfect holiness but only had words of fear, like 'taboo'. A way was found, however: God's high name stands alone, above all other names. Kingdom, too, is complex until we understand it as our deep longing for God to come and rule over us. Praying for our daily bread is familiar to Christians in poor communities. Where bread is not eaten, we may say 'rice' or just 'food'. In one Aboriginal community, we struggled to find a word for 'forgive'. We thought deeply about forgiveness and listed possible words like remove, throw away, cover, or untie. In the end we all knew it was to untie, to release us, to set us free: a dangerous translation, asking God to free us from our sins in the way we release the sins of others. Luke's final phrase was less difficult. Everyone in the world knows what sin is and the power of temptation: 'Don't let us go down the track to sin.'

Lord of the narrow way, don't let us go to sin but, when we do, release us, free us to follow you once more along the path to eternal life.

[1] Collect for Ash Wednesday, *Book of Common Prayer*, 1662

BIBLE IN A YEAR: **Ezekiel 30,31; Psalms 123–125**

Luke 11:5–13

God Hears our Prayers

'I am weak, but thou art mighty; / hold me with thy powerful hand. / Bread of heaven, bread of heaven, / feed me now and evermore, feed me now and evermore.'[1]

These parables belong with the Lord's Prayer. The disciples ask Jesus to teach them how to pray. Jesus doesn't give them a magic formula. Instead, he teaches them about the nature of God: not a distant, transcendent being but their heavenly Father who knows and cares about them. We must not overanalyse this parable, or indeed any parable which Jesus does not specifically interpret. Jesus did *not* say that God resembles the neighbour who will grant our requests if we persist enough, nor even that God resembles the kindly father who will give us whatever we want. What Jesus did say was that if an earthly man will get out of bed to help his earthly neighbour and if an earthly father responds kindly to his children, how much more can we, who pray to God as our heavenly Father, count on God's readiness to hear us and to answer.

Jesus encourages us, therefore, to pray in the knowledge that God cares about us, knowing how desperately we need God and knowing that God will listen to us. We must not ever, as some do, take these sayings to mean that we can presume upon God, presenting God with a blank cheque on which to write our requests. These assurances after the Lord's Prayer assume that those who ask, seek or knock, because of their need, are also yearning to know God's will and are longing for God's kingdom to come. We may be anxious about the necessities of life, our needs and our families' needs, but Jesus calls us to lift our eyes beyond this life: '...seek his kingdom, and these things will be given to you as well. Do not be afraid ... for your Father has been pleased to give you the kingdom.'[2]

Lord of our lives, thank you that you know our needs and hear our prayers. Help us to glimpse your coming kingdom, where joy will surpass all earthly pain.

[1] William Williams, 1717–91, 'Guide me, O thou Great Jehovah' [2] Luke 12:31,32

BIBLE IN A YEAR: **Ezekiel 32,33; 2 Peter 1**

Luke 11:14–28

Lord of the Flies?

'I bind unto myself today / the power of God to hold and lead, / his eye to watch, his might to stay, / his ear to hearken to my need.'[1]

First-century Judaism was intrigued with angelic and demonic beings. *Beelzebub*, 'Lord of the Flies', was an old and deliberately insulting misspelling of *Beelzebul,* 'Lord Prince', the full title of the Canaanite god Baal.[2] By Jesus' time, these titles were used for the ruler of the demonic world rather than *Satan*, which is not a real title but simply means 'adversary'. Jesus had healed the mute man by the very 'finger of God' (v 20), a sign that the kingdom of God was present in Jesus, foreshadowing the ultimate defeat of the adversary and the coming of light and wholeness. However, lurking in the crowd were powerful people, Jesus' adversaries. Under the influence of the ultimate adversary, they committed the ultimate sin. They declared good to be evil, that Jesus' powers were satanic. Jesus responded that if he were aligned with Satan, exorcising a demon would be mutiny. The strong man's fortress, Satan's fortress, falls only when attacked by an even stronger force. In the exorcism, two kingdoms have clashed. The stronger kingdom, God's kingdom, has defeated the kingdom of the evil one.

We are part of this battle and there can be no neutrality. Even the expulsion of evil by the finger of God is not enough! Even if God has healed, cleansed or forgiven us, we still must act to replace what God has taken away with whatever is good and godly. A young Christian man I know well was taken over by the evil of drug addiction. He put himself through a Christian rehabilitation programme and all seemed to be going well when he slipped back into a dark place. Now he is in an even worse state than he was before. If we have been delivered from .evil, we must fill that void with the life of God's kingdom, lest evil fill it again.

Lord of the spiritual realm, when dark powers assail us, deliver us by the finger of God and enable us to fill all our emptiness with you and your kingdom.

[1] Patrick, c389–461, tr CF Alexander [2] 2 Kings 1:2,3; historically complex: van der Toon et al, *Dictionary of Deities and Demons,* EJ Brill, 1995

BIBLE IN A YEAR: **Ezekiel 34,35; 2 Peter 2**

Luke 11:29–36

Darkness Cannot Overcome

'Good is stronger than evil; love is stronger than hate; light is stronger than darkness; life is stronger than death. Victory is ours, through him who loves us.'[1]

We still follow the conversation after Jesus healed the mute man. Jesus' adversaries, who had labelled the healing satanic, were silenced. The curious crowd asked for another 'sign' (v 29), but what they wanted was entertainment, tempting Jesus to perform a magic trick. Although they did not know it, three long years earlier, hungry and isolated in the desert, Jesus had resisted that same temptation, refusing to turn stone into bread, rejecting for ever the temptation to use his divine power for his own good or to impress others. No wonder Jesus' response has a hint of anger. He will not resort to showmanship. The only sign they will get is the 'sign of Jonah'. The Gentiles of Nineveh repented at Jonah's preaching. Jesus' preaching, by word and action, would be the only sign given to this Jewish generation, a clear sign to those whose minds were not darkened.

Jesus' sayings about light may seem disconnected. Some scholars wonder if Luke put them there for want of a better place. Perhaps Jesus did say these things elsewhere, but Luke is telling us something by his placement. The good news of the kingdom of God must not be hidden. If the kingdom of God is within us, we radiate its light. This was a powerful metaphor. Luke was a physician at a time when it was thought that our eyes emitted light and that we could see when that light met the light outside us. Those out of whose eyes shines the light of the kingdom of God are spiritually healthy, but the darkened eye indicates inner darkness, under the control of the evil forces of darkness. We whose eyes see and reflect the kingdom of God have the promise: the light which entered the world with Jesus shines in the darkness and the evil forces of darkness can never overpower it.[2]

Lord of the light, fill our whole beings with the light of the kingdom of God, that we may reflect that light into the darkness of the world.

[1] Bishop Desmond Tutu, 1931-2021 [2] see John 1:5

BIBLE IN A YEAR: **Ezekiel 36,37; Psalms 126–128**

Meaningless Ritual

'God has spoken by his prophets / spoken his unchanging Word, / each from age to age proclaiming / God the One, the righteous Lord.'[1]

The Pharisee wanted to hear more from Jesus, but got more than he bargained for. The stage was set for confrontation when Jesus declined the ritual washing – not declining hygiene, like refusing the Covid hand sanitiser! Jesus was refusing to participate in the Pharisees' pre-meal ceremony in which washing was not about cleanliness but supposedly making everything – people and utensils – ritually clean. Such fastidious routines were a mockery of true spiritual health. The Pharisees even tithed portions of their herbs and spices to obey the smallest detail of the law, but they were still unclean, like someone unwittingly stepping on a grave.[2] Reducing obedience to God to a plethora of minute rules, they neglected justice and mercy. The prophets had long ago railed against this spiritual blindness: 'I hate … your religious festivals … Even though you bring me burnt offerings … I will not accept them … But let justice roll on like a river'.[3]

We too must be aware of empty ritual. Kneeling, raising hands, even singing are not acceptable to God unless they spring from humble and merciful hearts.

The lawyers probably regretted that they had joined the confrontation. Jesus castigated them, as privileged people with scriptural learning who perpetuated the spiritual blindness of their religious predecessors. Abel and Zechariah (v 51), the first and last murder victims in the Hebrew Scriptures,[4] symbolised all the innocent dead of the past. The addition of the 'apostles' (v 49) opens the image to future martyrdom. The lawyers held in their hands the key to God's kingdom but, blind to it, they could not recognise the kingdom in Jesus nor assist others less privileged than themselves to see it. This is a stern warning to those of us who hold the responsibility of interpreting the Scriptures to others.

Lord of your written Word, help us always to seek you and find you in its pages and to share truthfully with others its news of you and your kingdom.

[1] George Wallace Briggs, 1875–1959 [2] Num 19:16–18 [3] Amos 5:21–24
[4] Gen 4:8; 2 Chr 24:20,21; Matt 23:35

BIBLE IN A YEAR: **Ezekiel 38,39; 2 Peter 3**

Psalm 72

The Primordial Messiah

'Most blessed, most glorious, the Ancient of Days, / almighty, victorious, thy great name we praise.'[1]

Has there ever been a leader so illustrious, so victorious and so magnificent as in this psalm? Among these proclamations of glory are hopes for the qualities we wish world leaders would display today, but which few attain – upholding justice and righteousness, helping the weak and marginalised, protecting the oppressed and needy. Psalm 72 was written for a coronation, possibly by David for the coronation of his son Solomon. It contains the exaggerated language traditionally used at coronations. In my youth, before Australia changed its national anthem, we sang 'God Save the King', calling upon God to give him victory over his foes, to make him 'glorious' and to give him long life. I have just watched British athletes mouth those very words about Queen Elizabeth on the Olympic podium.

Although Psalm 72 originated as a celebration of this earthly king, its lyrics dare to touch eternity. This king's name will outlive the sun. This monarch will be eternally revered. Although the time-bound Jewish monarchy ended, the psalm lived on because of this eternal dimension, the hope of a holy and just regime which would last for ever. Verse 17 is quoted in the *Talmud,* the ancient Jewish interpretation of Scripture, as proof that the name of the Primordial Messiah, the Christ before time, was known before the universe began and will live beyond it into eternity.[2] For Christians, verses like this leap from the pages of Scripture. We understand that Jesus, the true Messiah, was not just *known about* before time but *existed* before time. We also know that the Messiah became human. A king was born in Bethlehem, whose origins were 'from of old, from ancient times',[3] that is, *from eternity*. Jesus rightly named himself the Primordial Messiah – 'before Abraham was born, I am!'.[4]

Lord of eternity, thank you for caring about me. Lead me safely through the perils of this world. Thank you that, when life ends, you will grant me eternal life.

---

[1] Walter Smith, 1824–1908, 'Immortal, invisible, God only wise' [2] *Talmud Bavli,* Nedarim 39b [3] Mic 5:2
[4] John 8:58

BIBLE IN A YEAR: **Ezekiel 40,41; 1 John 1**

Denying my Lord

'Take up your cross and follow Christ, / nor think till death to lay it down; / for only those who bear the cross / may hope to wear the glorious crown.'[1]

The 'yeast of the Pharisees' (v 1) was hypocrisy, a trait which, allowed to grow, deforms our characters. Not all Pharisees were bad people – remember Nicodemus and Joseph of Arimathea[2] – but many believed that meticulous observance of rules and rituals earned favour with God, differentiating them from other people. All our secret thoughts and double standards will eventually be exposed for all to see. Yet the Pharisees own revered Scriptures declared that God, who inhabits eternity, also dwells with people who are 'contrite and lowly in spirit'.[3]

We read the grim words which follow, knowing that Christians were already facing persecution and martyrdom. Earthly powers could *only* harm the body, whereas God has power over our eternal future. I write '*only* harm the body' with trepidation. Can I boast, like Peter, that I would never fail my Lord?[4]

Threatened with the torture and death of me or my family, dare I say I would never yield? If I do, however, then one day, on the threshold of heaven, I will be deeply ashamed 'before the angels of God' (v 9). In that terrible moment, suspended between death and eternity, surely I will find that Jesus has already forgiven me and he will let me in. '...a word against the Son of Man will be forgiven' (v 10) is a message of grace for those who falter under persecution. What then is the sin 'that will not be forgiven'? As a boy, I asked my father. He said that anyone who worried about it certainly hadn't committed it! It was, he said, a conscious lifetime rejection of the Holy Spirit's pleading to come to God through Jesus. We can stumble, we can fall, even deny our Lord, but when the quiet voice within calls us back to him, we rise to follow him again along the path to eternity.

Lord of life and death, if ever I deny you, may I hear the Spirit calling me back. Give me the strength to take up my cross, seeking eternal life.

[1] Charles Everest, 1814–77, 'Take up your cross' [2] John 3:1; 19:38,39; Luke 23:50,51 [3] Isa 57:15 [4] Luke 22:33

BIBLE IN A YEAR: **Ezekiel 42,43; 1 John 2**

Luke 12:13–21

Eat, Drink and be Merry

'Take my silver and my gold, / not a mite would I withhold.'[1]

On the surface, this parable is about amassing wealth and relying too much on it. Almost a cliché, 'eat, drink and be merry for tomorrow we die' has entered our consciousness in literature and language. This seemingly simple story, however, is far from simplistic. The answers to the question, 'What was the rich man's folly?' are many and complex – and they still pervade human society.[2] *Preoccupation with possessions.* Until God interrupts the fool's self-congratulatory musings, there is nothing to the story but the man and his possessions. When his materialistic life was laid bare before God, however, it was actually empty. His possessions possessed him. *Security in self-sufficiency.* The fool comes across as deluded, thinking he needs no one else. His wealth will take care of him. He feels no need of the security of family, friends or community. He does not even need God. *The grasp of greed.* The fool's deepest thoughts reveal no compulsion to use his wealth to help those in need. Greed has eaten away at any compassion he may once have had. *The futility of pleasure-seeking.* The fool's dream is to spend his life gratifying his whims and pleasures. The greatest good he can imagine is his own self-indulgence.

Sadly, this attitude is only too common today, an approach to life which has been called 'practical atheism'.[3] The rich fool, a first-century Jew, believed in the existence of God but, in practice, lived as if there were no God, particularly a God who might make demands of him. The rich fool's dreams sound surprisingly like many people's retirement plans! Among Australians, seventy per cent believe God exists, whereas only seventeen per cent actually attend a place of worship. Even practising Christians can spend too much time and energy on their material lives and their future comfort and security.

Lord of my future, help me to use my resources responsibly in this world, conscious of the needs of others. Thank you that my future is secure with you.

---

[1] Frances Havergal, 1836–79, 'Take my life' [2] RA Culpepper, 1995, p257
[3] Peter Jones, *The Teaching of the Parables*, Broadman, 1982, p127–141

BIBLE IN A YEAR: **Ezekiel 44,45; Psalms 129–131**

There is More to Life

'We rest on thee, our shield and our defender. / We go not forth alone against the foe. / Strong in thy strength ... in thy name we go.'[1]

Jesus often used vivid hyperbole to make his point. He does not mean that we must never be anxious, never have concerns about anything at all. A parent should be anxious about a sick child. We should all worry about the coronavirus. Jesus himself was worried about what would happen to the disciples after he left them[2] and he agonised about the unimaginable horror of the cross.[3] There are, however, two keys in the passage to understanding exactly what Jesus meant. First is his opening word, 'Therefore' (v 22). Luke intends us to understand that Jesus' words immediately follow the parable of the rich fool, a crucial connection spoiled by a heading in my Bible. We must not allow ourselves to become like him, preoccupied with material things and selfish pleasure. As Jesus frequently points out, the more we possess, the harder that becomes. Following Jesus awakens our consciousness to the spiritual dimensions of life. When the rat race of materialism starts to control us, we must remember Jesus' words: 'life is more than food, and the body more than clothes' (v 23).

The second key is in Jesus' conclusion, where he lifts our thoughts of earthly life into an eternal dimension. As Jesus' 'little flock' (v 32), we need not be afraid, no matter what happens to us. Do not forget that Jesus' words, 'Do not be afraid', were spoken when he was on the way to his cross and his followers were on the path to persecution and death. Of course we fear pain, but beyond pain and death lies eternity. God cares about us and about our ultimate future. The God of the universe, the Creator of stars and galaxies, cares even about birds and flowers. God knows their lives and takes pleasure in them. This same God is *pleased* to give us the kingdom.

Lord of the needle's eye, to whom all things are possible, forgive us when we value material things. Help us to discern the still small voice. Take us to eternity.

[1] Edith Cherry, 1872–97, 'We rest on Thee, our Shield and our Defender' [2] John 17:11–19 [3] Mark 14:32–36

BIBLE IN A YEAR: **Ezekiel 46,47; 1 John 3**

Luke 12:35–48

Plucked from the Fire

**'We have followed too much the devices and desires of our own hearts ...
We have left undone those things which we ought to have done'.[1]**

We begin with one of Jesus' most recognisable themes: he will return unexpectedly. Jesus uses the well-known first-century understanding of the servant-master relationship. Jesus will return suddenly, bringing history to a close and ushering in the new order. We must be ready for God's new kingdom. Two thousand years of waiting dulls our sense of expectation, but we must be alert, living in eager anticipation of the life to come.

From this simple teaching, Jesus shifts the master/servant metaphor into one of Scripture's most difficult themes: the notion of different levels of punishment.[2] Envisaging how individualised punishments might be applied is purposely hidden from us. The future holds mysteries which we cannot know. Our limited minds cannot contain the mind of God. Puzzling over punishment, the medieval church revived the old idea of 'purgatory', a place where people destined for heaven were made holy before being allowed in. While I don't believe in the grim purgatory of the medieval painters, I cannot ignore Jesus' warnings. I cannot avoid the disturbing truth that I am one who dares to teach and lead the church. I have been 'entrusted with much' (v 48) and I will be 'judged more strictly'.[3] Heaven holds only peace, joy and freedom from all pain and distress. Will this stricter judgement happen before I enter God's eternity? Paul told church leaders that those who built people's faith on lasting foundations will be rewarded. Those who did not, whose work lacked permanence, would also be saved but only as people 'escaping through the flames'.[4] Do any of us deserve heaven? Like John Wesley, perhaps we should think of ourselves as 'a brand plucked from the fire'.[5] Jesus will take us to heaven, but some of us will have questions to answer before we get there!

Lord of the judgement, we confess our failings. You are our Redeemer and Judge. Forgive our sins. Have mercy on us. Open the gate of heaven and let us in.

[1] The Confession, *Book of Common Prayer* [2] Cf Matt 10:40–42; 16:27; Rev 22:12 [3] James 3:1 [4] 1 Cor 3:15 [5] Cf Zech 3:2

BIBLE IN A YEAR: **Ezekiel 48; 1 John 4**

Understanding the Times

'God of grace and God of glory, / on your people pour your power … Grant us wisdom, / grant us courage / for the facing of this hour.'[1]

How tragic that the gospel of peace should not bring peace but conflict. Inexorably, Jesus' final journey takes him to Jerusalem. He knows well the 'baptism' (v 50) that awaits him: he will be plunged into torture and pain that will engulf him until death. He knows, too, that his followers will soon face their own baptisms of fire. Their choice to follow him will bring persecution, torture and martyrdom; dividing family, community and nation. Jesus wishes that the fire were already kindled. As a man, contemplating the agony ahead, he wants it over with. He also wants the Christian struggle in the world to begin, so that it too can finally end. That long struggle still continues two thousand years later. Somewhere today, Christians will die for their faith. Somewhere today, a church will be torched. Jesus was indeed born that there might be peace on earth, but it will not happen until he returns to establish the new world order. That we must still await, not sleeping but watching, eager for it but wise about the times we face.

Not yet at Jerusalem, Jesus speaks to a rural crowd, seemingly critical, as if addressing religious leaders. Those leaders will face judgement, but ordinary believers cannot afford complacency. Rural communities could predict the weather but the people, even though they had come to hear him, had not discerned the signs of 'this present time' (v 56). Perhaps they had not cared enough about the corruption of their religious leaders. Perhaps they had not discerned that the old religion needed to be renewed from within. Most seriously of all, they had not interpreted Jesus' signs and words that he was the foretold Messiah and that God's new kingdom was at hand. Today, church leaders can still err, but that does not excuse other Christians from complacency nor from the struggle to live the values of the kingdom.

Lord of history, help us read these difficult times, to discern right from wrong and to demonstrate the life of your kingdom to a desperate and suffering world.

[1] Harry Emerson Fosdick, 1878–1969, 'God of Grace and God of Glory'

BIBLE IN A YEAR: **Daniel 1–3; Psalms 132–134**

Luke 13:1–9

Suffering of the Innocent

'Turn your eyes upon Jesus, look full in his wonderful face, and the things of earth will grow strangely dim, in the light of his glory and grace.'[1]

News travelled south along the road from Galilee: Pilate had committed a gruesome massacre. Although this is not recorded elsewhere in our Scriptures, Pilate was notoriously violent towards religious gatherings he considered subversive.[2] From Jesus' 'answer' (v 2), it seems that the crowd were questioning whether these deaths were deserved, whether Pilate was God's instrument of punishment. Some interpreted the old covenant as teaching that good people were blessed and bad people cursed, but this atrocity picks up another strand in the Old Testament: the difficult question of the suffering of the innocent. This is the only context in the Gospels where Jesus deals specifically with innocent suffering. His answer is clear: those people had not suffered because they were worse sinners than others. Turning to a natural disaster, the collapse of a tower in Siloam, possibly part of the wall of Jerusalem, Jesus gives the same answer: It was an accident, with no connection to the victims' sins. Christians who want to see the hand of God in tsunami and flood and drought, or even in the Covid virus, should heed Jesus' words.

We live in a fallen world where God permits human sin and corrupted earth to run their course. Both will continue to mutate and deform. Both will cause suffering and death, until God brings this age to its close and creation is finally restored. Jesus warns us that, when confronted with news of such disasters, we should be thoughtful, reminded of our own mortality, using the opportunity to repent – that is, to turn our lives around and reorient ourselves to the right path.[3] Like the fig tree, we always have another chance. However, like the fig tree's reprieve, that chance does not last for ever.

Lord of the earth, we feel the pain of sin and a dysfunctional world. Help us to turn and follow you, who will make all things new.

---

[1] Helen Lemmel, 1863–1961 [2] Eg Josephus, *The Antiquities of the Jews*, 18:86–87 [3] Greek: *metanoia*, 'turn around', 'repent'

BIBLE IN A YEAR: **Daniel 4,5; 1 John 5**

Staying Close to God

'Be near me Lord Jesus, I ask you to stay / close by me for ever and love me I pray ... fit us for heaven to be with you there.'[1]

Psalm 73 begins the third set of psalms. Almost the numerical centre of the book, it is the theological centre, looking back as a synopsis but marking a shift to a more questioning attitude. Psalm 72 ends with a paean: 'may the whole earth be filled with his glory. Amen and Amen.' But so does the very final psalm: 'Let everything that has breath praise the LORD.' Psalm 73 reinforces the major message which flows through Psalms 1–72, that godliness does not mean relying upon our own strength or resources, but relying on God: what the psalmists constantly called 'taking refuge' in God.[2] In Psalm 73, however, a questioning note enters. Why do the wicked prosper? Why doesn't God act?

The psalmist's Scripture was the Torah, in which it was unquestioningly proclaimed that God's curse upon the unrighteous was both immediate and tangible:

'Your basket and your kneading trough will be cursed ... your womb ... the crops ... your herds'.[3] In the psalmist's experience, in contrast, the 'wicked' were healthy, happy, strong and carefree (vs 3–12). Envy of them almost destroyed him (vs 2,3). Was it all an illusion? Had he kept his heart pure for no purpose? (v 13). Then somewhere, perhaps in the Temple itself, the psalmist found 'sanctuary' (v 17), a place where he could face himself and how he was acting before God: 'I was a brute beast before you' (v 22). He saw that nothing on earth should matter to him but God. His flesh and heart may fail, but God would never fail him (v 26). Fleetingly, his mind reaches for the answer in an unnamed eternity: 'afterwards you will take me into glory ... my portion for ever' (vs 24,26). Finally, he knows that God is all he needs: 'it is good to be near God' (v 28).

Lord of all, forgive me for the times I doubt you, losing my faith. Thank you for never failing me. All I want is to know you are near me.

---

[1] Anon c1885, 'Away in a Manger' [2] The word 'refuge' occurs in 32 of the first 72 psalms: eg Pss 2,5,7,9,11,16,25,46 [3] Deut 28:16–19

BIBLE IN A YEAR: **Daniel 6,7; 2 John**

Luke 13:10–17

Healing the Whole Person

'O Sabbath rest by Galilee! / O calm of hills above, / where Jesus knelt to share with thee / the silence of eternity, / interpreted by love.'[1]

When I was aged 12, the newspaper began a Sunday edition. Dad refused it. I was angry because they moved the comics from Saturday to Sunday. Dad ignored my plea to give up Monday instead, as it was printed on Sunday! The Sabbath rest was decreed for the wandering Israelites to recoup spiritually and physically. The rules were simple – everyone knew what work was. By Jesus' time, religious leaders had invented complex, oppressive rules but even they would untie their donkey. In modern, technological society we must attend to more than thirsty animals on Sunday. Even my father turned on lights and drank tap water! We want the internet, sewerage, TV and emergency services. Obeying the spirit of the Sabbath is difficult today but the principles still stand. All human beings need time to recuperate spiritually, mentally and physically. The stress of the Covid pandemic shows how crucial this is.

The woman's story is usually taken as another of Jesus' healings, but is it more than that? Women have not been thought significant. I believe Jesus consciously chose to heal her in a public place. He grants her redemption and wholeness, thereby offering the kingdom to all women who are demeaned, denied their proper status and oppressed by society. Disabled at many levels, hers is the story of many women. She had been bound by Satan for 18 years (v 16) and her condition demanded compassion. Jesus healed her, Sabbath or not. Jesus doesn't say that Satan singled out this woman to suffer disability. She was a victim of the world's fallenness, in which evil forces have power to hurt people, to deceive, to deform and to destroy. We pray in the Lord's Prayer that God will deliver us from the evil one[2] – and that is what God will do. At the end of time, God will destroy evil for ever.

Lord of the Sabbath, deliver us from the evil one. Help us to revive our spirits and renew our minds as we navigate our way through a fallen world.

[1] John Whittier, 1807–92, 'Dear Lord and Father of mankind' [2] Matt 6:13

BIBLE IN A YEAR: **Daniel 8,9; 3 John**

The Narrow Door

'There was no other good enough / to pay the price of sin. / He only could unlock the gate / of heaven and let us in.'[1]

Like yeast in a batch of bread dough or the small seed that grows into a tree, the kingdom of God grows from small beginnings, but Jesus' band of followers, walking the dusty backroads of Samaria, could not see it yet. It was becoming less clear to them that following Jesus would lead to anything significant. They had eagerly left all to follow him, but doubts were arising in their minds. They were small and vulnerable. There were even rumours that Jesus' life was in danger. Was this it? Was this dusty and travel-weary group all that the Jesus movement would achieve? Jesus had promised them eternal life. Were only a few people going to make it? The question prompted a very stern answer, one which we must take to heart: the door to eternal life is narrow, entry is restricted and one day it will be closed.

Jesus does not explain why the door is open to some but not others. Over the centuries, numberless preachers have thumped their pulpits, thundering their pronouncements of what will keep us out of heaven, but Jesus does not say here. What does Jesus say elsewhere about who might be excluded? Those who do evil?[2] Those who don't feed the hungry or clothe the naked?[3] Those who enjoy their comfort and ignore their needy neighbour?[4] Those who don't believe in the Son of God?[5] Perhaps it is best if, like Luke, we let Jesus' words retain their mystery and ambiguity. What we know for certain is that entry through the door is entirely up to God and that there will be surprising reversals. We must never presume upon God's grace. We must strive to live as if heaven depended entirely on how we lived our lives, but we always know that, in the end, everything depends on God's grace.

Lord of the narrow door, we have fallen short. We do not merit heaven. We relinquish ourselves entirely into your hands. Open the door to us and let us in.

[1] Cecil Frances Alexander, 1818–95, 'There is a green hill far away' [2] Matt 13:41 [3] Matt 25:41–43 [4] Luke 16:19–26 [5] John 3:18

BIBLE IN A YEAR: **Daniel 10–12; Psalms 135,136**

Luke 13:31–35

Old Jerusalem and New

**'Lo! He comes with clouds descending, / once for favoured sinners slain ...
Hallelujah, Hallelujah, Hallelujah! God appears on earth to reign.'[1]**

Jesus' words are ominous. His fate and Jerusalem's fate are inextricably linked. Zion, the city of God, where stood the Temple enclosing the sacred Ark of God, should have been the place where God's name dwelt[2] and from where God's glory spread outwards into the world. Instead, it had decayed from within, fallen into ungodliness, succumbed to foreign empires and tolerated the rise of a corrupt religious leadership. Jerusalem had ignored and even killed God's messengers – prophets such as Uriah, Zechariah and those killed by Jezebel.[3] Now Jerusalem was about to kill her own Messiah, not at the hand of Herod but on the orders of a pagan overlord, manoeuvred by the religious leaders. Jesus knew that it would not be long before that same foreign empire would annihilate the city, leaving not one stone standing upon another.[4]

Mount Zion is probably in sight by now. Jesus is overcome by a complex of emotions, undoubtedly including dread of what he must first endure, but here his feelings are dominated by his sorrow about what might have been but now would never be. He longs to gather the people, to enfold and protect them, to be their Saviour now, but they did not want him. Shortly, he will enter the city. A few chapters on, my Bible heading says 'Triumphal Entry', but that is a product of centuries of colourful Palm Sunday rejoicing. The entry was pitiful. Jesus' small band of followers tried to make something of it. They shouted 'Blessed is he ...'[5] – but Jerusalem did not shout. Jerusalem would crucify him. After his ascension, the world would not see Jesus again, not until he returns to usher in the 'new Jerusalem',[6] that is, the eternal kingdom of God. Then we will truly shout, 'Blessed is he who comes in the name of the Lord!'[7]

Lord of eternity, eagerly we await your return. Forgive our doubts. Cleanse us of our sins. Make us fit for your kingdom. We will greet your coming with joy.

---

[1] Charles Wesley, 1707–88 [2] 1 Kings 8:29 [3] Jer 26:20–23; 2 Chr 24:20,21; 2 Kings 21 [4] Luke 19:44
[5] Mark 11:9 [6] Rev 21:2 [7] Mark 11:9

BIBLE IN A YEAR: **Hosea 1,2; Jude**

Jeremiah 35–52

YAHWEH REJECTS HIS PEOPLE

The final 18 chapters of the book of Jeremiah tell the sorry tale of Judah's descent into political, religious and social degeneracy, leading, in fulfilment of ancient warnings, to exile. Moses warned the Israelites that if they spurned the covenant, the land would thrust (vomit) them out into exile. Jeremiah tells the story of the obduracy of the last king, Zedekiah, whose pig-headedness is captured (36:19–26) in his act of burning the prophet's scroll containing the word of God.

Although popular religion was thriving, along with days of fasting and large gatherings in Jerusalem, the hearts of the king, the people, the priests, the official prophets and the nobility were not attentive to the authentic word of the Lord through Jeremiah. Jesus, in the parable of the sower, warned against hard-heartedness: the inability to allow the word of God to seep deeply into the inner being so as to bring about a rich harvest. Jeremiah's generation refused to heed the word of God and they went into exile.

The sovereignty of the Lord, his freedom to speak and act freely in any situation, is a major theme. Above all the significant human players – Babylon, Egypt, the Medes and Persians and all the little nation states nestling in the fertile crescent – sits the Lord, whose word alone is final. The Lord uses any human instrument he chooses, but that does not validate any and every act of callousness, cruelty or indifference. All human beings are held accountable to him.

Jeremiah challenges us to follow the example of David, not those of most of the other kings of Israel and Judah. It is said of David that his heart was after God's own heart[1] and that he served the Lord in his generation.[2]

Joe Kapolyo

FOR FURTHER READING

Walter Brueggemann, *A Commentary on Jeremiah: Exile and Homecoming*, Eerdmans, 1998
JA Thompson, *The Book of Jeremiah*, NICOT, Eerdmans, 1980

[1] 1 Sam 13:14 [2] Acts 13:36

Jeremiah 35

Hear, Understand and Obey

Lord, teach me to a be a good listener. May I fully digest what I hear with understanding, letting your word be firmly rooted in my heart.

We do not know much about the Rekabites, except that they were nomadic Kenites, who drank no alcohol and had rejected a settled lifestyle complete with houses, agriculture and urban dwelling. The group Jeremiah encountered descended from a certain Jehonadab, son of Rekab, who was once associated with Jehu's purge of the household of Ahab.[1] Jehonadab issued the commands which defined his descendants' identity and to which they continued to adhere unwaveringly two centuries later.

Under instructions from the Lord (v 2), Jeremiah tests the resolve of the Rekabites. They were unmoving, proving their loyalty and obedience to their ancestor. This encounter provided Jeremiah with an object lesson for the nation of Israel and their king, who had abandoned the word of the Lord and indulged in Canaanite worship and culture. Their unfaithfulness stood in sharp contrast to the constancy of the Rekabites and attracted God's severest censure.

In our modern cultures all over the world, we admire self-made men and women, people like Jeff Bezos, Elon Musk and Bill Gates. That is why Frank Sinatra's song, 'I did it my way', is so popular at funerals, certainly in England. By contrast, Israel as a community was meant to be a people steeped in listening to what the Lord had said in the Torah and continued to say through his prophets. Disciples of Jesus are under the same obligation. The decisions and choices we make, the identities we create for ourselves, should conform to and grow out of our understanding of the ways of the Lord – and that demands deep listening.

Develop an unwavering devotion to the word of God through daily hearing, reading, studying, meditating and memorising. 'Let the message of Christ dwell among you richly'.[2]

[1] 2 Kings 10:15 [2] Col 3:16

BIBLE IN A YEAR: **Hosea 3–6; Revelation 1**

The King Burns God's Word

Thank you, Lord, for the gift of hearing. Help me to receive your word with understanding. Let me hear the cries of the needy and respond in obedience.

The past two years have been tumultuous. The world has been convulsed by the Covid-19 pandemic and the effects of climate change. Personal lives have been devastated by loss of loved ones, livelihoods and environments. Similarly, Jeremiah's world was shaken by regional political and military conflict from the end of the seventh century BC. Egypt had been shattered by the Assyrians in the battle of Carchemish and was therefore unable to offer Judah any protection. Into this turbulent situation, God spoke through his prophet (vs 1,2) just as, no doubt, he is speaking into our troubled times through his word. Which of us is listening and what is our response?

God hoped that the king, the prophets, the priests and the people would heed his words and repent (v 3), so that he might forgive their sins. Sadly, overall the word fell on deaf ears. For his part, the king not only destroyed the scroll but he also sought to arrest the originators, to kill them (v 26).[1] The king and the nation had placed themselves outside the covenant of God. Why had they bothered to call a fast (v 9) if they had no interest in what God had to say? Popular religion was thriving – although only a few had any time for God.

Speaking truth to power is not without its dangers, although it has to be done. For his troubles, the king received fearsome condemnation; his dynasty would cease and he himself would die in dishonour. The word of God will not go away simply because we ignore it. One day, it will hold us to account before God.

'Trust and obey, for there's no other way to be happy in Jesus, but to trust and obey.'[2]

[1] Cf Jer 26:20–23 [2] JH Sammis, 1846–1919, 'When we Walk with the Lord'

BIBLE IN A YEAR: **Hosea 7,8; Psalms 137,138**

Attention to God's Voice

Teach me to accept your word, however inconvenient.

'When elephants fight, the grass gets hurt.' This evocative African proverb captures the fate of the little nation states, in the ancient Near East, nestling along the fertile crescent, from the Euphrates-Tigris river systems, down the Jordan valley to the Nile delta. Power struggles tended to involve the superpowers, Assyria, Babylonia and Persia to the north and Egypt to the south. The period between 598 and 587 BC, during the ineffectual reign of Zedekiah, demonstrates this predicament. The king was allied to Egypt and desperately hoped that his strategy would bring him peace and security, but to no avail. The official propaganda in Jerusalem supported this ideology, but Jeremiah had a very different opinion, based on God's word.

Jeremiah's prophetic stance and his opposition to official policy did not endear him to the rulers. Under false premises (v 13) they arrested him, beat him up and threw him into a horrid jail, where he was sure to die (vs 16,20). He was later moved, at the intervention of the king, to a more agreeable environment (v 21). The king, desperate to have Jeremiah and the word of God on his side, supporting the official ideology, sought audience with the prophet twice (vs 3,17). Jeremiah, however, was uncompromising: the word of God contradicted the status quo and predicted defeat and surrender to the Babylonians.

Zedekiah and Judah's problem, a problem with which we are all too often familiar, was their lack of attention to the word of God (v 2). The king sought urgently to change the will and word of God to fit in with his desires – but we must always remember that God is not always on our side.

God is on his own side. We, however, may choose to join him on his side. That requires paying close attention to his word.

BIBLE IN A YEAR: **Hosea 9,10; Revelation 2**

Rise up, God, and Save us

Lord, you call us to the obedience of faith. Teach us to be faithful to that calling.

The Covid-19 pandemic has wreaked havoc all over the world. Millions have died. Many communities have been devastated. Personal livelihoods have been destroyed and countries fallen into great debt. This pandemic is symbolic of many other disasters that befall human beings, personally and collectively. There are tsunamis, floods, earthquakes and hurricanes – not to mention war. We look to the future with a sense of trepidation because of climate change and environmental degradation. However, we still have hope in God our Saviour.

Psalm 74 reflects the physical, mental, emotional and spiritual conditions of the exiles in the immediate aftermath of the destruction of Judah in 587 BC. Israel's enemies had ripped the heart out of the nation: the Temple at the centre of its universe. The destruction was total, with every valuable item stripped, removed and carried away as plunder along with the exiles taken into slavery. The situation was bleak. The nation lay in ruins and the people descended into spiritual hopelessness. Furthermore, God was silent – or so it seemed.

This lament gives expression to deeply felt anguish and seeks to rouse the nation to place their confidence in the God who alone is able to come to their aid. He has proved his power to save in the past. After all, he is their King, Creator and Redeemer, who silenced Pharaoh, overcame the Red Sea, the River Jordan and all other obstacles, in order to plant his covenant people into their Promised Land. His anger, which has led to the present circumstances, was roused by their faithlessness. God can be trusted to do again what he has done in the past.

What difficulties are you confronted with? Use this lament to give expression to your pain and to awaken faith in the God who alone can intervene on your behalf.

BIBLE IN A YEAR: **Hosea 11,12; Revelation 3**

Jeremiah 38

Seeking Godly Leaders

Lord, thank you for all our civic, national and international leaders. May they always lead in righteousness and the fear of God.

Think of some leaders you are familiar with: parents, teachers, captains of commerce and industry, civic and other political leaders. Distinguish between excellent and poor examples. What is it that makes the difference between them?

In this passage, we have one example each of good and poor leadership – and the consequences. On the one hand we have Ebed-Melek and on the other King Zedekiah. Ebed-Melek enters the narrative abruptly. He is an Ethiopian (a Cushite), a black man, in the service of King Zedekiah. There were many Ethiopians in the Egyptian army, which was allied to Judah against Babylon. That is why many think of him as some high-ranking military attaché (the description of him as a Cushite has falsely led many traditional commentators to suggest that he was a slave, but the ease with which he approaches the king and rebukes him and his nobles in public contradicts this notion). Ebed-Melek shows good leadership: he is decisive and he uses his considerable diplomatic influence to reverse a gross injustice and thereby rescues Jeremiah from certain death. He sees the injustice done to Jeremiah and he rebukes the king's complicity in the scheme. As a result, he saves the prophet's life and the Lord promises him rescue from the Babylonians.[1]

King Zedekiah, on the other hand, shows poor leadership, which leads to the capture of Judah and the deaths of many people. His leadership is based on the shifting sands of fear: fear of his officials, the Babylonians and even the Jews who had already defected to the enemy (vs 5,19). What he does not do, is fear the Lord enough to listen to his word and to do it. That is the thing that Jeremiah consistently declares in his hearing.

Identify injustices, systemic or sporadic, in your community, where you should be exercising godly leadership to curb evil.

[1] Jer 39:15–18

BIBLE IN A YEAR: **Hosea 13,14; Revelation 4**

Resist God at your Peril!

Dear Lord, teach me to walk in your ways so that I may not live in fearful expectation of judgement.

It is futile to resist the will of God. Jeremiah had consistently laid before king and country two possibilities: submit to Babylon and live, or resist and die. Those who submitted – Jeremiah (and Baruch) and Ebed-Melek – lived, whereas all who resisted – the king, the royals, the Jerusalem establishment and most of the population in Judah – perished.

The end came in July 587 BC. The Babylonian field commanders took their seats in the Middle Gate. At their sight, the cowardly king, along with his sons and nobles, fled, heading for the Jordan Valley with the hope of escape. They abandoned the very people on whose behalf they had put up such resistance. However, like their resistance, their flight was futile. They were all captured and presented before Nebuchadnezzar at his field headquarters in Riblah. There the nobles and the king's sons were executed. Zedekiah's eyes were gouged out. The last thing he saw and would see as long as he lived, was the annihilation of the Davidic dynasty. He was then shackled and led to Babylon where he died in ignominy.

By contrast, there are two salvation oracles: the first is for Jeremiah (vs 11–14) and the second is for Ebed-Melek (vs 15–18). Jeremiah had consistently criticised and resisted the official anti-Babylon viewpoint. He was arrested and imprisoned. Ebed-Melek, in a daring display of courage, had opposed the king and his complicity in Jeremiah's plight. These two men, under God's favour, escaped with their lives and are singled out as the bridge into Jewish exile and the faith that would survive it. One of them was a black African.

However countercultural God's word may appear, it is the gateway to life: '...the wages of sin is death, but the gift of God is eternal life'.[1]

[1] Rom 6:23

BIBLE IN A YEAR: **Joel 1,2; Psalm 139**

Jeremiah 40:1 – 41:15

Dangers of Disobedience

Dear Lord, in times of confusion, give me eyes to see where you are working and wisdom and courage to align myself with your will.

In history, when two powers or ideologies clash, even when there is an outright winner, there is confusion in the immediate aftermath. Jeremiah had been freed under imperial orders.[1] Then he was rounded up again, shackled and prepared for the gruelling journey to Babylon. In Ramah, the imperial commander, Nebuzaradan, recognised him, freed him and supplied him with resources (40:5b,6). In the end he recommended that Jeremiah join Gedaliah, the newly appointed Jewish governor of the Babylonian province of Judah. In this confusion, God does not lose sight of the welfare of the individual. When you feel overwhelmed by circumstances, remember the Lord is still in control and has not forgotten you.

The words of 40:1 promised a message from the Lord through Jeremiah. Surprisingly, the prophecy comes from the mouth of Nebuzaradan, a pagan commander of the conquering army (vs 2–6). He gives the theological reason for Judah's demise as covenantal unfaithfulness: Judah's refusal to obey God. How is it that a pagan gets hold of this theological truth, which Jeremiah had been proclaiming all along, but not the king, his nobles or most of the people of Judah?

Gedaliah, a man of noble descent, established his administration. He would represent the people to the Babylonians, and the people in return should live productive lives. The results in the first year were encouraging but the remnant, even after they were free to settle in the land, refused to accept the 'submit to Babylon and live' ideology from God. They remained recalcitrant and so went into a tailspin resulting in more bloodshed. Gedaliah was assassinated and many more people died (41:1–9).

Ask the Lord to give you spiritual insight, through his word, so that you may discern where he is active and align yourself with him.

[1] Jer 39:14

BIBLE IN A YEAR: **Joel 3; Revelation 5**

The Exodus Reversed

Dear Lord, as I read your word, give me clarity of insight that I may understand and obey your judgements on matters that affect all life.

In the aftermath of the Babylonian conquest of 587 BC, the social and political situation in Judah was fluid and chaotic. There were coups, countercoups and assassinations. The only constant feature was God's word. Jeremiah insistently taught the people that if they submitted to Babylon they would live. This message had proved to be a stumbling block to the kings and nobles before the Exile and also to the remnant in the immediate aftermath of the Exile.

The remnant gathered in a solemn assembly (42:1–3), reminiscent of covenant-making occasions,[1] and formally asked Jeremiah to seek God's guidance for the future of the community. They pledged to obey whatever the Lord revealed, however unpalatable (v 6). In response, the Lord set before the people two alternatives, reiterating what Jeremiah had been saying all along. First, 'If you stay in this land, I will build you up … Do not be afraid of the king of Babylon … I am with you and will save you and deliver you from his hands' (vs 10,11). Second, 'If you are determined to go to Egypt … the sword you fear will overtake you there, and the famine you dread will follow you … You will be a curse and an object of horror, a curse and an object of reproach' (vs 15–18).

The whole assembly with one voice rejected God's word. They declared Jeremiah to be a liar, not sent by God (43:2). The people disobeyed the word of the Lord and, in a reversal of the Exodus, they returned to Egypt dragging the unwilling Jeremiah with them.

God's will is not always palatable. Ask the Lord not only to reveal his truths, however inconvenient ('unfavourable', 42:6), but also to give you courage to obey without question.

[1] See Exod.24:3,7

BIBLE IN A YEAR: **Amos 1,2; Revelation 6**

Jeremiah 44,45

God-is-Dead Theology

Lord, please sharpen my faculties of perception so that I may hear and see you more unmistakably in your word, so that I may dwell in your presence for ever.

A clash of ideologies comes to a head: obedience to the Lord, as Jeremiah advocates (and has done all along), or allegiance to the Queen of Heaven, as the exiles adamantly assert. Those two options are still on offer today: do we choose to follow God in Christ or will we cling to other idols or ideologies?

In the light of the exiles' adherence to the religion based on allegiance to the Queen of Heaven, Jeremiah sets before them an object lesson from recent history. Judah fell and went into exile because of idolatry and if they, the Jews in Egypt, persisted in those idolatrous practices, they too would suffer the same fate. Jeremiah's words fell on deaf ears, just as they had done over the past forty years. In fact, they countered with their own strange evidence, saying that it was precisely

because they had abandoned idolatry (presumably under Josiah's reforms) that the disasters of 587 BC had come upon them. Therefore, in word and deed, they determined to follow other gods.

In choosing stubborn resistance, they removed themselves from the protections and blessings of the covenant and opted instead to suffer the wrath of God and come under the fearsome curses so clearly spelt out in 44:26–28[1] and so clearly demonstrated in the recent fall of Jerusalem. The exception to this wholesale destruction was Baruch (ch 45). Because he supported Jeremiah's cause, the Lord would preserve his life just as he had preserved Caleb and Joshua's lives and promised to preserve the life of Ebed-Melek.[2] God rewards obedience and punishes defiance.

When a person decides to reject God, they place themselves outside the reach of his help, to their tragic loss.

[1] Cf Deut 28 [2] Num 14:30,38; Jer 39:16–18

BIBLE IN A YEAR: **Amos 3,4; Psalms 140,141**

The Lord Alone is Sovereign

Though populist dictators rise to power and natural disasters and climate change threaten human existence, the fact remains that the Lord is sovereign and I will trust him.

Chapters 46–51 of Jeremiah contain oracles to the nations.[1] Such messages show Israel's conviction that the Lord rules over all the nations. Egypt comes in for censure because it resisted God's determination to free Israel from slavery, was steeped in idolatry (46:25) and stood against the pro-Babylon ideology of Jeremiah and Baruch.

The year is 605 BC. The Egyptian army, under Pharaoh Necho, had a base at Carchemish on the banks of the River Euphrates. They were routed by the Babylonians and the onslaught followed the retreating army back to Egypt. The Egyptian soldiers who had been so full of confidence are in disarray and hastily retreat. The carnage is total. The soldiers and their allies are regarded as sacrificial animals (vs 20–21), a frightened snake fleeing in haste (v 22) or a devastated forest (v 23), chopped and stripped as by locusts (v 23). This is God's vengeance on Egypt. It does not stop at the battle ground. It goes all the way back to the civilian population in the cities of Egypt, who must go into exile (v 19).

Jeremiah portrays the fortunes of Egypt and of all the nations as orchestrated by God (v 10). He alone is sovereign. Babylon does not have the last word on either Egypt or Israel, but the Lord does (vs 25–28). Both Egypt and Israel will be rehabilitated when Babylon has itself been punished.

In the light of this emphatic statement of the sovereignty of God, what are we to make of current world trends? We may not have answers to these questions, but we can remember that the Lord is sovereign, he is in control.

When we are bewildered, confused and often hurt by mega world trends and events, let us ask the Lord to give us confidence to trust him and his judgements.

[1] Cf Isa 13–23; Amos 1,2

BIBLE IN A YEAR: **Amos 5,6; Revelation 7**

Psalm 75

God Holds the Future

When tempted to despair because of circumstances far beyond my ability to control, dear Lord, help me to rest my hope and confidence in you, our Maker and Sustainer.

During the Babylonian Exile, God's people were in despair. They were without hope, in bondage, stateless and scattered from Egypt to Babylon. Kingship had disappeared. The prophetic voice was dim and the priesthood and its cultic apparatus were irrelevant. Could there still be a bright future, full of hope? Psalm 75 sounds a clear note of confidence.

In 2022 we too can empathise with the plight of ancient Israel. Many today are stateless: the refugee highway is huge. Even for the most developed of nations, the burden of debt is crushing. Climate change and its consequences threaten to destabilise the natural order as we have known it. Under these circumstances, it is easy to fall into despair and a sense of hopelessness. This psalm speaks to us a message of hope, just as it did to Israel.

The psalm starts with a declaration of thanksgiving to God whose 'Name is near'[1] and whose wonderful deeds of salvation, such as the Exodus, indicate his presence and activity among his people. God is portrayed as the Sovereign Judge whose judgements are impartial. He is also the Sustainer of his creation. Yes, we must exercise good stewardship over his creation, but its ultimate fate and that of its inhabitants are in his hands. Neither the Babylonians to the north nor the Egyptians to the south have the final word. That prerogative belongs to the Lord. This God, to whom alone belongs ultimate judgement, will make all his enemies drink the wine of his wrath to the dregs. This is the confidence we have in the midst of destabilising circumstances.

Remember what the Lord has done in history and in your own life. From such knowledge, you will draw comfort, encouragement and hope in times of difficulty.

[1] See also Deut 4:7

BIBLE IN A YEAR: **Amos 7,8; Revelation 8**

Human Gods are Unreliable

Lord, please deliver me from constructing my security on the shifting sands of false premises, politically, ideologically or theologically. Give me wisdom to distinguish between falsehood and the truth.

From time to time, men and women make speeches that change the course of history. Martin Luther King's speech in Washington DC on 28 August 1963, led directly to two pivotal Civil Rights Acts that transformed the fortunes of millions of African Americans. Jeremiah 48 is similarly powerful in determining the fate of Moab. The Lord is Sovereign. His utterances, cast into stone, for good or ill, determine the futures of the objects of his decisions.

The Lord's declaration starts with a list of six of the most important cities of Moab: Nebo, Kiriathaim, Heshbon, Madmen, Horonaim and Luhith (other towns are added – see vs 21–24). The 'Woe' (v 1) announces distress, death and God's judgement. Moab's centres of power, security, influence and safety – and their populations – have been weighed in the balance, found wanting and destined for destruction. The destruction by Nebuchadnezzar (580 BC) will be catastrophic and will spread to the valleys, plains and hills (vs 8,9). Complacent Moab, likened to undisturbed wine (vs 11–14), will be poured out.

The other object of the Lord's wrath is Chemosh, the Moabite god and his priests. They, too, will go into exile. Both Judah, who trusted in Bethel, and Moab, whose people trusted in their own strength and in Chemosh, will be thrust out into exile. Although the human agent of this destruction is Nebuchadnezzar, the true originator of the judgement is God. Ultimately, all nations and human beings will have to give an account before God. He is the final judge. Blessed is the nation, man or woman whose trust is in the name of the Lord.

Every day, competing ideologies seek our allegiance. Influencers try to persuade us to buy into their lifestyle remedies. Be wise in choosing who or what you trust.

BIBLE IN A YEAR: **Amos 9; Revelation 9**

Jeremiah 48:26–47

Moab is Totally Shattered

Lord, the fortunes of all the nations and all their people are in your hands. Teach me to surrender my life to you and lead others to do the same.

Moab is totally ruined and its destruction is described in many vivid metaphors. Its demise is territorial, social, religious and economic. In its heyday, Moab was famed for overweening pride, conceit and arrogant self-admiration. It was offensively contemptuous, boastful and idolatrous. It did not take God into its reckoning. It defied God and ridiculed Israel. Therefore, it faced God's total judgement. It is described as a despised drunk wallowing in its own vomit (v 26). It has lost its status, its land; it is homeless and stateless. Its military strength drains away as in childbirth, in its defencelessness it is picked on and shattered as if it was a discarded clay jar. Its famed vine groves and the wine that formed the basis of its economic success are ruined by God through his agent Nebuchadnezzar, who is likened to a bird of prey (v 40).

The destruction is so total that Jeremiah is moved to mourn with Moab (vs 32,36). The nation's immediate future is bleak, with nowhere to turn; terror, snare, pit and exile are its only choices. 'It is a fearful thing to fall into the hands of the living God.'[1] However, in the midst of judgement, God remembers mercy and so promises to re-establish a remnant in Moab (v 47).

The reasons given for Moab's harsh judgement are, first, that its people defied God (v 42) and, second, that they ridiculed Israel for no reason (v 27). The Bible makes it clear that there is only one God, the Lord (whom we know as the Father of our Lord Jesus). Therefore, worship of any gods, like Chemosh, and other forms of idolatry are defying God and incur his wrath.

Every person and nation will give account of themselves to God and receive his unbiased judgement. In Jesus, God has given a way by which we may be saved.

[1] Heb 10:31, AV

BIBLE IN A YEAR: **Obadiah; Psalms 142,143**

There can be no Escape

Lord, please give me the wisdom to realise that resisting your will is futile. Your sovereign resolve affects our individual destinies and also international political and cultural strategies.

I was born in Northern Rhodesia (which became Zambia in 1964) at the height of the power of the British Empire. I experienced first-hand the indignities and humiliations of being on the wrong side of the insatiable appetites for power and wealth that fuelled the European colonial enterprise. I often reflect on that period in my personal and my country's fortunes. Jeremiah's depiction of the experiences of little countries, like Edom, that, nestled in the Jordan Valley right down to the Gulf of Aqaba, may throw some light on my reflections. In this passage (vs 7–22) we focus on Edom's fortunes, in a list that also includes Ammon, Damascus, Kedar, Hazor and Elam, when faced with Babylonian imperialism. All these countries faced the same threats and outcomes, although each had its peculiar reasons that explained the intervention and ultimate viability. Edom descended from Esau, Isaac's firstborn and Jacob's twin brother.[1] There were tensions between the brothers, signalling the future relations that would define their nationhood later. The Edomites were famed for their wisdom. They were territorially, intellectually and economically secure, but their fortunes were about to change dramatically in the face of Babylonian expansion. Behind the Babylonian ambitions was the hand of the Lord, Edom's ultimate enemy. Edom, like Sodom and Gomorrah, cannot escape, just as sheep and shepherds are powerless before a lion or small animals before a powerful bird of prey. The destruction of the Edomites would be total and proverbial. There was, however, one sign of hope (v 11): the defenceless would find succour in the mercy of God.

God's actions in history raise unanswered questions. It is clear, however, that all who suffer, including from racial discrimination in a white world, can find comfort in his mercy.

[1] Gen 25,27,28,32,33

BIBLE IN A YEAR: **Jonah 1,2; Revelation 10**

Jeremiah 50:1–28

From Hero to Villain

Lord, in my desire to do your will, teach me to respect the limits of your delegated authority, so that I may always serve you 'in the fear of God'.[1]

While working for 11 years in a pastorate in north London, I became familiar with the phrase, 'We do not talk to Babylon'. Babylon is used as a byword for injustice, cruelty and oppression: the perception of most young black people in that context of the police (remember the murder of George Floyd by a police officer in Minneapolis in May 2020). This reputation of and label for the police are derived from ancient Babylon and its fearsome character expressed in injustice, brutality and oppression.[2]

Jeremiah's pro-Babylon preaching tells us that initially Nebuchadnezzar and his army were instruments in the hands of God to punish rebellious Judah, just as Assyria had been used a century earlier to punish Israel. Babylon exceeded its mandate, however, turning cruelty, injustice and oppression into ends in themselves. That is why a massive publicity campaign was called for and mounted, to tell everyone that Babylon too will be captured (vs 2,21–28). Babylon had rejoiced exceedingly as it pillaged other nations, reducing them to ruins, nations whose security had been undermined by the will of God (vs 11–13,17). A coalition of the Medes and Persians from the north would devastate Babylon (vs 9,14–16). Babylon's key colonial policy was to conquer, capture, deport and disperse. The Medes and Persians would reverse these policies and return people to their homelands (vs 18–20).

In history, empires rise and fall: Assyrians, Babylonians, Persians, Greeks, Romans, modern Europeans and others. Jeremiah makes it clear that history is not random. Its forward movement is not just historical but theological. God, the only Sovereign, will have the last word.

All authority on earth belongs to God. He delegates it to people, institutions and nations. In recognition of this fact, all leaders must lead in the fear of God.[3]

[1] 2 Cor 7:1, AV [2] See Hab 1:6-11 [3] 2 Sam 23:3,4

BIBLE IN A YEAR: **Jonah 3,4; Revelation 11**

Danger from the North

Dear Lord, when I am in the depths of hopeless despair, help me to know for certain that there are no limits to your willingness or power to save.

For a long time Babylon was the foe from the north, summoned by the Lord to chasten Judah and the surrounding nations. Now, in a reversal of fortunes, it is Babylon which will bear the brunt of the chastening by the Lord at the hands of a foe from further north: an invincible army, a coalition of the Medes, Persians and mercenaries from their vassal states (v 3). The day had come for Babylon to be filled with fear, consumed as in a fire, cut down by the sword, plundered and made desolate so that no self-respecting human beings would choose to inhabit it (vs 39,40). But why? What did Babylon do to become the enemy of the Lord?

Babylon became arrogant, led astray by false prophets and idolatry. It had not recognised that its power had been delegated from the Lord, the Holy One of Israel (v 29) and, like Pharaoh of old, it oppressed Israel and refused to set its people free (v 33). In its arrogance, Babylon did not take account of Israel's Redeemer (*go'el*), the divine role akin to the human next of kin whose duty it was to avenge the killing of a loved one or redeem a relative and their property from slavery; this Redeemer is so strong that no shepherd (king) can stand against him (v 44). Just as the Lord had redeemed Israel from slavery in Egypt through Moses, so now he would repeat that feat by saving Israel from Babylonian exile in a second exodus. So, although Israel was in dire straits, it could always depend upon its Kinsman Redeemer, the Holy One of Israel, to come to its people's aid and liberate them. In Jesus, that Kinsman Redeemer, with his inexhaustible resources, is available to us.

The Lord graciously allows us to share in his mission to bring the world to the obedience of faith. Let us not take this privilege for granted nor become arrogant.

BIBLE IN A YEAR: **Micah 1–3; Psalm 144**

I am Against you, Babylon

As I pray, 'your will be done',[1] help me to align all my being, faculties and energies with your will so that I may always only serve your purposes.

Why has Babylon, once a 'gold cup' (v 7) in the Lord's hand, now become an object of his wrath? How is it that the once prominent 'pro-Babylonian' ideology in Jeremiah's preaching has been turned on its head? Then, Jeremiah had insisted that submission to Babylon was the Lord's will and the only way for survival.[2] Nine times in four verses the Lord repeats that with Babylon ('you') 'I shatter' nations and kingdoms, armies, societies, leaders and their followers (vs 20–23). Now, however, the fury of the Lord's anger is focused on his once preferred instrument. Why?

It is scary to read what the Lord has purposed to do to Babylon. He has determined to destroy Babylon: 'I am against you' (v 25); and 'I will stir up the spirit of a destroyer against Babylon … I will send foreigners … to winnow her … in the day of her disaster' (vs 1,2). Babylon was that tall spreading cedar with fantastic boughs under which all the nations of the world came to shelter. Now they are all urged to 'Flee from Babylon! Run for your lives!' to avoid getting caught up in its destruction (v 6). The downfall of Babylon was to be so terrible that there could be no healing for it. All this has come about because the Lord Almighty, the Maker of all things, against whom all idols are powerless, the Portion of Jacob, is bringing all his resources to act on behalf of Israel, the tribe of his inheritance. The chastening of Israel by Babylon was to purify it, but Babylon became arrogant, proud and conceited, forgetting that it too must give account to the Lord, who alone is Sovereign.

In everything that the Lord assigns to us, it is his will alone that matters. Let us, then, like Jesus, always say, 'not my will, but yours be done'.[3]

[1] Matt 6:10 [2] Jer 38:1,2 [3] Luke 22:42

BIBLE IN A YEAR: **Micah 4,5; Revelation 12**

God is Sovereign in Salem

We pray for all authority figures, role models and influencers. May they conduct themselves in righteousness and the fear of God, so that all people everywhere may live in peace.

On 1 September 2016, Colin Kaepernick, an African American football player, 'took the knee' instead of standing to attention during the singing of the national anthem, at the start of a game. This was a personal gesture to protest against racial discrimination, which is a denial of a fundamental human right. The gesture has since gone viral, and most English professional football players and officials take the knee at the start of each game. The search for justice, peace and equality is universal and enduring. There have been many declarations of principle and concomitant gestures, but the search goes on. The objective, however, is still out of reach.

Psalm 76 points to the only solution: the King of [Jeru]Salem (the word means peace; cf shalom, Solomon, salaam).

It is out of Zion that this God, the Lord, has revealed himself. The world owes an immense, eternal debt to Israel for preserving the self-revelation of the Lord. He is described in terms that depict him as the warrior king, whose awesome majestic power, located in the Temple in Zion, overcomes all pretenders, local, national or cosmic, and their offensive weapons. His power overwhelms and restrains the oppressors but saves and raises up the oppressed (v 9). His acts of salvation are legendary, not least the Exodus from Egypt led by Moses. His dynamic word has power to create and to overpower. This King is Judge over all the earth (vs 7–9). Through Jesus Christ, he has demonstrated his commitment to promoting and protecting well-being and the ability to flourish for all human beings everywhere (vs 12), especially the poor and downtrodden.

It is not enough to say that I am a person of peace who does my neighbour no harm. We must be proactive in combating every outrageous incidence of injustice.

BIBLE IN A YEAR: **Micah 6,7; Revelation 13**

Jeremiah 51:33–64

Speaking Truth to Power

Dear Lord, raise up an army of fearless prophets who will declare your word to every person in this generation: young and old, rich and poor, prince and pauper alike.

At first glance, there is a level of absurdity in this passage, as there would seem to be throughout the book of Jeremiah. We have an obscure and unofficial prophet of a tiny nation whose God seems to have been crushed and his Temple stripped, his people either killed or taken into slavery in exile. The survivors feel confused, disgraced, insulted, ashamed, as if they had been swallowed up by some giant snake, digested and then regurgitated because their Temple lies in ruins (vs 34,51). Babylon and its idols have triumphed; the Babylonians feel secure and inviolable. And yet, and despite apparent evidence to the contrary, Jeremiah dares to speak authoritatively to the emperor of the world's superpower, saying that the God of Israel will turn the tables on Babylon and destroy it. Unimaginable, but true. The destruction will be complete; the society and its leadership will disappear; and the army, the buildings and even the protective wall will all collapse and lie desolate. Indeed, Babylon will be 'an object of horror and scorn, a place where no one lives' (v 37).

Jeremiah's confidence to speak truth to power lies in the fact that the God of Israel is none other than the Lord Almighty, the Creator and Sustainer of all things. He is sovereign and speaks authoritatively into any and every situation. Besides, the Babylonians had dared to slaughter and thus destroy his people Israel (v 49), from whom the desire of all ages, the Messiah of all the earth, would later be revealed. What the Babylonians declared as acceptable colonial strategies of the empire have been recast as genocide, with grave consequences.

Tragedies (personal, national or international) can destroy hope. God, however, is neither powerless nor indifferent. Appeal to him and he will surely act.

BIBLE IN A YEAR: **Nahum 1–3; Revelation 14**

The Dawn of Redemption

Thank you, Lord, for your constancy in all the turmoil of life.

Moses warned the Israelites that breaking the covenant made with the Lord carried serious consequences.[1] Sadly, the inevitable happened, just as Jeremiah had been at pains to point out. The last mention of the Lord in this book is to underline the fact that the fall of Jerusalem, following the evil deeds of the people – especially their kings – forced the Lord's hand to thrust them out of Israel (v 3). The events that led to this outcome are rehearsed in the rest of the chapter (vs 4–30).[2] The popular demand for a king, opposed by Samuel,[3] eventually brought the nation to its knees and brought about an almost irreversible end of this pillar of nationhood. The destruction of the Temple, the deportation of the most able people and the political machinations of power-hungry survivors undermined any hope of the survival of the nation. At his call, the Lord indicated that Jeremiah would continue to prophesy, to deaf ears, until the whole nation went into exile.[4] And so it proved to be. However, with the release of Jehoiachin (v 31), there is a slight glimmer of hope of redemption.

In the midst of the great turmoil that engulfed the ancient Near East during Jeremiah's time, when empires rose and empires fell and there were huge movements of populations from their traditional lands, there was one constant, the voice of the Sovereign Lord. At the beginning of the third decade of the 21st century, when traditional securities are under threat and powerful movements are on the rise, it is easy to despair. We should remember Jeremiah, who focused on the word of the Lord God Almighty. In him we have constancy and to him we look with renewed hope for a new dawn.

It is hard to find a more turbulent period than Jeremiah's. We have our own challenges today but, through them all, the Lord remains constant. That is our hope.

[1] Deut 29:14–28 [2] Cf 2 Kings 24,25 [3] 1 Sam 8 [4] Jer 1:4–19

BIBLE IN A YEAR: Habakkuk 1–3; Psalm 145

Scripture Union

By purchasing *Encounter with God*, you are helping to support Scripture Union's mission with children and young people. Thank you!

Subscribe to our free supporter and prayer magazine at su.org.uk/ connectingyou

REVOLUTIONARY JOY

Philippians is many people's favourite book of the Bible and it's easy to see why. It's a privilege and a joy to expound this wonderful letter for *Encounter with God*. Advent and Christmas are many people's favourite times of the year, including mine, so the joy is doubled! Expect to be encouraged as we journey through a letter and a season that are so full of life, light and wonderful, irrepressible joy.

Yet Philippians should deeply challenge us too. I believe some commentaries and expositions of the epistle are too peaceful, lacking a cutting edge. True, Paul affirms much that is positive about the Philippian church, but he also has some strong things to say. As I wrestled with the text, I concluded that it's more challenging than we often realise. Paul urges his readers to grow in righteousness (1:9-11), stand firm on the gospel (1:27), repair broken relationships (4:2,3), practise radical contentment (4:12,13) and much else besides. Above all, he directs us to look to Jesus and live like him (eg 2:5). He models following Christ wholeheartedly, showing us what this looks like in practice. He sets a high standard; big challenges come in verse after verse. Philippians is full of joy, but if we truly understand what Paul is saying we will recognise that his message – and example – are revolutionary.

If we want the joy that Paul has, we need to take on board the message of this letter and live like he does. The 'solid joys' of which Philippians speaks are only attained, as the hymn reminds us, by pursuing the 'lasting treasure' of the gospel.[1] The extent to which we experience the joy that bursts from this extraordinary epistle will depend on how far we give ourselves to our Lord and his purposes for us. Over the next two weeks, may God deepen our commitment and at the same time fill us with 'joy unspeakable'.[2]

Peter Morden

FOR FURTHER READING
Gordon D Fee, *Paul's Letter to the Philippians*, Eerdmans, 1995

[1] John Newton, 1725–1807, 'Glorious things of thee are spoken' [2] 1 Pet 1:8, AV

Philippians 1:1–11

True-Love Ways

As you begin this journey through Philippians, ask God to remind you of old truths and show you new things from his Word.

Love is at the heart of Christianity, so we are not surprised when Paul prays for the Philippians' love – *agapē* in Greek – to 'abound more and more' (v 9). This sounds simple, but it needs thought. Contemporary understandings of love are often wrong-headed and Christians may have mistaken notions of what it means to be loving towards others. Someone might say, for example, that it's wrong to challenge a non-believer to turn to Christ or to urge fellow disciples to press on in holiness. Rather, so the argument runs, we should 'just love' – which often betrays a desire to please people rather than God. This is not showing *agapē* love as the New Testament defines it.

Notice how verse 9 ties love closely together with 'knowledge' and 'depth of insight'. Gospel knowledge and gospel wisdom should shape our practice of love. For example, a proper knowledge of the gospel will lead us to share it with others; if we truly love non-Christians we will surely speak, since Jesus is their only hope. Similarly, if we have a clear insight into God's purposes we will urge other Christians to pursue holiness. This will not be done harshly but graciously and supportively, for we are fellow pilgrims with struggles of our own. Love, knowledge and wisdom are closely intertwined, informing and enriching each other.

This is a high standard of love. How can we attain it? The answer is through – and only through – the power of God (v 6). Paul 'yearns' (see v 8, ESV) for the Philippians with a deep 'affection'. Whence is this affection derived? Only from Christ himself (v 8). He shows us both the standard and the source of Christian love. Knowing such *agapē* love is an urgent need in both church and world. Who will you love today?

Commit to pray regularly for a non-Christian to come to Jesus. This may happen quickly but may not! Do we love them sufficiently to keep praying?

BIBLE IN A YEAR: **Zephaniah 1–3; Revelation 15**

Philippians 1:12–18a

Gospel Growth

Lord Jesus, thank you that you embody what it means to live a generous life. Thank you for giving everything for me on the cross.

Paul is in chains simply because of his commitment to preach the gospel. Almost certainly he is in Rome: his reference to the 'whole palace guard' (v 13), the praetorian guard, is to the elite soldiers stationed in Rome. It is quite possible that Paul's imprisonment at the heart of this powerful empire will end in execution (cf vs 19–21). He is in grave danger.

In this situation, how does Paul pray? I know how I would pray: fervently to be released! Not Paul, though. He rejoices in a new freedom that others are already experiencing, namely a greater liberty in gospel preaching (v 14). He does this even though some preach to 'stir up' trouble for him (v 17). Their actions could plunge him into even deeper difficulty, yet such is his passion for Christ that his own predicament pales into insignificance beside his burning desire to see the gospel proclaimed.

What is our attitude to kingdom growth, when we see it bursting into life? Perhaps another church in our neighbourhood is growing and drawing people away from our own fellowship, or someone is preaching the good news in new ways and – seemingly – with wrong motives. Of course we should ask questions of others' gospel work – Paul certainly does. Yet our overriding response should still be joy that the kingdom is advancing. I confess that pastors like myself are the worst at this, often too concerned about growth in our own churches to rejoice in the fruitfulness of others! These verses call us to repent and to celebrate kingdom growth wherever it occurs. A secondary application is to carry that generosity into the whole of life and be glad when others are successful. Let's be generous, for in so doing we reflect the heart of God.

Think of a church in your area that is growing. Rejoice in all that God is doing and pray that their outreach in the run-up to Christmas is fruitful.

BIBLE IN A YEAR: **Haggai 1,2; Revelation 16**

Philippians 1:18b–26

Matters of Life and Death

Thank you, Father, that because of your love for me in Jesus, death will be the gateway into your eternal presence.

The Russian revolution in 1917 ushered in a wave of communist uprisings which swept the globe and helped shape the history of the 20th century. Yet the reality of communist government failed to live up to the ideals and much misery resulted. What was needed was a different type of revolution. At least some recognised this. One early communist was overheard saying, 'I used to read the New Testament. It is the most wonderful story ever told. That man Paul. He was a *real* revolutionary. I take my hat off to him!'[1]

Our verses today show us the revolutionary Paul and the New Testament message which made him so thoroughly radical. On one level, what he says is not hard to understand. He is faced with two possibilities: life or death. He believes he will be released because he reckons his work as an apostle is not yet completed. Even so, he is torn (vs 22–24).

He longs to be with Christ which is 'better by far' (v 23). Ultimately, verse 21 reveals Paul's heart. He is determinedly focused on Christ.

This may seem simple to understand, but it's staggering when we truly comprehend it. Can we say the words of verses 21 and 23 along with Paul? Our answer to this question will depend on whether we really believe the gospel as he did. Jesus died and rose again and if you have trusted him you are eternally secure. Do you *really* believe this? Sometimes our theology is merely head knowledge. It has not permeated deep within, gripping our whole being. For Paul, biblical theology has so captured his mind and heart that he views all of life and death through a gospel lens. As a result he lives as a true revolutionary. May God strengthen us to do the same.

Pause and allow the challenge of this reading to penetrate deeply. Pray for a deeper understanding, so that Paul's words in verse 23 become your words.

---

[1] Mikhail Borodin, quoted in Peter Morden, *Message of Discipleship*, IVP, 2018, p171

BIBLE IN A YEAR: Zechariah 1,2; Psalms 146,147

Philippians 1:27 – 2:4

Courageous, Compassionate

'God in three persons, blessèd Trinity.'[1] Lift your praise to him who is one God, Father, Son and Holy Spirit, living in perfect unity.

Some commentators regard verse 27 as the key verse in the whole letter. Paul's overarching desire, expressed throughout Philippians, is that his readers 'conduct [them]selves' in a 'manner worthy' of Christ's gospel. This principle shapes all dimensions of daily life: nothing is held back. Throughout his letters, Paul teaches that inner thoughts,[2] friendships,[3] finances,[4] working lives,[5] service within the gathered church,[6] and much more, are all to be brought into conformity with the gospel. The psalmist prays, 'give me an undivided heart'.[7] Is there any part of your life which is somehow 'divided', partitioned off from the influence of the gospel? Begin to dismantle that wall today, in the strength that God gives.

In our verses, Paul especially brings the gospel to bear on the church. The word 'one' is crucial. It occurs four times, but the appeal to unity affects the whole argument. Note that this is not a lowest-common-denominator unity, which is shapeless and has no purpose. Rather, it is a gospel unity, closely reflecting the life and mission of the one who brought the church into being: Jesus Christ. Paul is especially concerned that God's people remain wedded to the core truths of the gospel, standing firm in a hostile world (vs 27,28). Further, he wants them to love one another in ways that are patterned on Christ's greater love for them (2:1). I write these words as we continue to move through the ravages of Covid-19 and navigate our way into a new future. Few things are needed more than gospel churches that are courageous in standing for the truth and are compassionate (v 1), embodying the love of Christ in community. Church is not always like this of course, but let's be part of the solution rather than part of the problem. What positive difference can you make?

What will it mean for you to 'conduct yourself' in a manner worthy of the gospel in your relationships as we anticipate the coming of Jesus?

---

[1] R Heber, 1783–1826, 'Holy, Holy, Holy, Lord God Almighty'   [2] 2 Cor 10:5; Phil 4:8; Col 3:2-5   [3] Rom 12:5; 1 Cor 1:10   [4] 2 Cor 9:6,7   [5] Col 3:23; 1 Thess 4:11-12   [6] 1 Cor 12:27-30   [7] Ps 86:11

BIBLE IN A YEAR: **Zechariah 3,4; Revelation 17**

Philippians 2:5–11

With us in the Valley

'Hark! the herald angels sing, / "Glory to the newborn King"'.[1] Spend time today worshipping your King, Jesus.

These verses are not often read at this time of year, yet they are perfect for Christmas Day. The passage is shaped like a deep, steep-sided valley. God's Son descends into the valley. The one who is in 'very nature' God becomes in 'very nature' man, a servant (vs 6,7). The phrases used by Paul show that Jesus wasn't pretending: the incarnation really happened. He was both fully God and fully man. If he had been born in a palace that would have been extraordinary enough; yet he goes even lower for he comes as a 'servant', born in a stable (more likely a cave)[2] in an outpost of the Roman Empire, wrapped tightly and laid in an animal's feeding trough, unable to feed himself, clothe himself or defend himself from attack. How the angels must have wondered and worshipped. Today let us join them.

There is even more, for Jesus descends further. He experiences death, a sinner's death on a cross (v 8)! The bottom of this valley is dark and lonely. However, this is not the end of the story, for God the Father lifts the Son out of the valley onto the heights through his resurrection and exaltation. These verses, sometimes known as the 'Carmen Christi' or 'Hymn to Christ', call us to worship him.

Even so, we easily miss Paul's overriding purpose. He writes not primarily to inspire us to praise. First and foremost, he wants us to live like Christ; we are to serve others in humility, as he did (vs 5,7). There may be an immediate application on Christmas Day; sometimes Christmas with extended family can be chaotic and tense! If this is your situation, may you reflect something of Christ. As you do this, remember that in his time God will lift you up too.

However you spend this most special day, know that Jesus descended into the valley for you. Bow before him, the incarnate Son of God.

[1] Charles Wesley, 1707–88, 'Hark the Herald Angels Sing' [2] The early church fathers, Justin Martyr and Origen, both believed this

BIBLE IN A YEAR: **Zechariah 5,6; Revelation 18**

Philippians 2:12–18

A Better Boxing Day

**'The Word became flesh and made his dwelling [tabernacled] among us.'[1]
Continue to praise God for the incarnation.**

The day after Christmas is known as Boxing Day in many countries. The name probably originated in Victorian Britain, where a tradition developed of 'boxing up' leftovers and giving them to the poor. Today, in the West, Boxing Day is often a time of greed not giving. People spend large amounts of money on commodities they don't need. None of this is said to condemn, but we are called to live differently, to 'shine … like stars' (v 15). We could do worse than revive the old Boxing Day tradition. Certainly, we should swim against the tide of consumer culture and think of creative ways we can do good to others.

However, Paul takes giving several steps further. He isn't sharing leftovers or even sharing liberally out of what he has. Instead, he offers his very self. The Philippians' service is described as a 'sacrifice' and his own life is a 'drink offering' poured out on top, making the first sacrifice complete (v 17).[2] Are we willing to give ourselves completely in service of God and of others? Such a question can seem too big for us, but we can start right now in myriad small ways, at work, at home and in the church. How is God calling you to offer yourself today?

Such self-giving is, astonishingly, a route to rejoicing (vs 17,18). Paul is able to celebrate because he is firmly focused on Christ and the 'day' of his coming, that is, his glorious return (v 16). He knows that on that day darkness will be dispelled and everything brought into the light. The challenge is to live our lives so that what will be important on that day is what is important to us now. Such an attitude may be derided by many, but it is the pathway to lasting joy.

'What can I give him…? … what I can I give him, / give my heart.' This Christmas time, offer yourself afresh to God.[3]

[1] John 1:14 [2] Cf Num 15:3–10 [3] Christina Rossetti, 1830–94, 'In the Bleak Midwinter'

BIBLE IN A YEAR: **Zechariah 7,8; Revelation 19**

Philippians 2:19–30

Soul Friends

Thank God for friends past and present, who have shown you the love of Christ and helped you to follow him more closely.

Our verses give us a window into Paul's world and, especially, the co-workers who faithfully laboured alongside him. First, there are the Philippians themselves. Paul had planted the church and continues to encourage them in discipleship, praying faithfully for them and longing to visit (v 24). Second, there are specific individuals: Timothy, who is like a son to Paul (v 22), and Epaphroditus, a key church leader at Philippi whose illness caused great distress (vs 26,27). In the West, we emphasise the individual rather than the corporate, but Covid-19 and the isolation it has brought has shown us afresh the importance of relationships. The New Testament shows us just *how* important. For Paul, the interests of Jesus Christ and concern for the welfare of others are almost the same thing: he moves seamlessly from one to the other (vs 20,21). If we are to live under the lordship of Christ, we need to have the same mindset. He created us for community.

The friendships revealed in this passage are rich and deep. Certainly, for Paul and Timothy, their mutual love was lifelong. We need Christian friends who are committed to us for the long haul. Seek out such relationships and, when you have them, invest in them. They are precious. Friendship is wonderful in and of itself, but our verses highlight something more. Timothy, Epaphroditus and Paul are great friends, but they don't merely enjoy one another's company – they engage in gospel work together, each making a unique contribution to the common cause. Some of the greatest friendships are forged in the heat of gospel ministry. Let us follow the example of Paul and his friends, and join together in the 'work of Christ' (v 30).

Spiritual friends are vital for accountability, gospel ministry and because friendship can be delightful! Who can you reach out to in friendship this Christmas time?

BIBLE IN A YEAR: **Zechariah 9,10; Psalm 148**

Wonder-working Power

What are the guiding principles that govern how you live? Reflect on these and offer them to God. Is there anything that he wants you to change?

Political parties publish manifestos before elections, setting out their principles and priorities. Verse 10 is essentially Paul's manifesto, his personal mission statement. Some translations and expositions suggest that the three dimensions of the verse – knowing Christ, his resurrection power and his sufferings – are essentially different, but this does not reflect the original Greek. The 2011 NIV gets it right by tying resurrection and suffering much more tightly to the overarching desire to know Christ. If we ask the question, 'How do we know Christ?' the answer verse 10 gives us is this: live a life that closely follows the contours of Jesus' own. We should serve as he did, knowing that, as we do so, suffering will surely come.[1] In this way, we will know Christ more. Paul's manifesto is a call for vigorous action.

Why is resurrection mentioned before suffering and death? They seem the wrong way round. The answer is most likely this: to live like Jesus we simply must have his power. The Greek word is *dunamis*, from which we derive English terms such as 'dynamic' and 'dynamite'. Only through the explosive power of Jesus' resurrection, released in us by the indwelling Holy Spirit, can we follow our Lord wherever he leads. Yet with that internal 'dynamic' at work, Paul's manifesto can truly become our own.

Philippians is a challenging book and today's passage is no exception. It's easy to feel that we are called to something unattainable. Yet that is not the case, for power is on offer. Perhaps you are facing an extremely tough situation. How will you cope? Or maybe you sense God calling you into something new and it's scary. Can you really step out in faith? It won't be easy, but there is power available and what amazing power it is!

Our aim should be to live in ways which cannot be explained apart from Jesus' resurrection power within us. Make it your prayer to live like this.

---

[1] Cf Phil 1:29

BIBLE IN A YEAR: **Zechariah 11,12; Revelation 20**

Philippians 3:12 – 4:1

Tender and Tough

Grace and truth. Thank God for these biblical qualities and the way they are displayed in the life of Jesus.

There is much in our world that is positive, which should fill us with joy and hope.[1] Yet there is much that is wrong too. Paul details some of the problems of his first-century world (vs 18,19). He could easily be writing about our own day, marred by materialism and consumed by consumerism, full of injustice and a lack of self-control, leading to 'shame' and brokenness (v 19). Sometimes as Christians we are loath to call these things out. We need clear, applied biblical thinking and the courage to speak prophetically when the situation demands it.

This is not all that is necessary, however. Sometimes we speak stridently, without love in our hearts. Paul shows us a better way, for when he speaks the truth he does so with 'tears' (v 18). He sees the tragedy of a society rebelling against God. He knows he has the answer: the cross of Christ. At the cross, people are delivered from the penalty and power of sin and broken lives are made whole. Yet, tragically, many live as its enemies, rushing headlong to destruction (vs 18,19). Paul speaks out but he also weeps, giving us a model of how to engage with our world.

One further thing is needed. If we are going to speak, even with love, we need to live in ways consistent with what we say. Awareness of our status as Christians helps us do this. It was a great privilege to be a Roman citizen, yet Paul knew that every Christian enjoyed an even greater privilege with which came great responsibility: we are citizens of heaven (v 20)! We are called to speak truth with grace, but we recall that Jesus embodied these qualities in the way he lived.[2] We most faithfully follow him when we do the same.

How has God challenged you about the words you speak, the way you speak them and the way you live? Respond to his challenge.

[1] Cf Phil 4:8 [2] John 1:14

BIBLE IN A YEAR: **Zechariah 13,14; Revelation 21**

The Antidote to Anxiety

Verse 6 encourages 'thanksgiving'. What are the things in your life you especially want to thank God for?

Recent years have seen much turmoil. Covid-19 has affected us all to some degree, but for you there may have been other struggles. Whatever your situation, there is much to feel anxious about. Verses 6 and 7 are like a doctor's note, prescribing the antidote to anxiety. On one level the prescription is simple: bring everything without exception to God in prayer. The words 'anything' and 'in every situation' are truly all-encompassing. These verses are very special to me and I know them by heart – though this doesn't mean I always put them into practice! Yet what a promise they offer when we do! God's peace can guard the castle of our heart, standing sentinel on the walls, stopping worries from breaking through. What further encouragement do we need?

We have additional weapons in our arsenals as we wage war against anxiety.

Another way we battle our fears is to concentrate our attention on all that is 'excellent' and 'praiseworthy' (v 8). It might be the innate beauty of creation, such as a wonderful view or exquisite birdsong, or it could be something lovely which humans, with all their God-given potential, have produced, such as a well-written book or great music. Ultimately, however, we are to think of Jesus and rejoice in him (v 4), for truth, nobility and all the other qualities mentioned in verses 8 and 9 are found supremely in him. With this change of focus we find that our worries are kept at bay; there is simply no room left for them, for God's peace and joy now reign supreme. This is the ideal of course! Nearly all of us struggle with fears at some time, so don't feel discouraged. Nevertheless, God has given us a wonderful prescription for anxiety. With his help, let's follow the remedy.

Put verses 6 and 7 into practice by lifting your anxieties to God, resolving to leave them with him. What positive things will you think about today instead?

BIBLE IN A YEAR: **Malachi 1,2; Psalms 149,150**

Philippians 4:10–23

Finance and Festivity

Thank God for the person who led you to Christ. Was it just one person or were there others supporting them, perhaps financially?

'I rejoiced greatly in the Lord' (v 10). By now we are not surprised that Paul says this. He's urged us repeatedly in this letter to rejoice.[1] As emphasised in the Introduction to these notes, he wants us to know 'solid joys'.[2] He feels it himself and knows how wonderful it is. He doesn't direct us to focus on joy per se, but on the reasons we have for rejoicing: we are 'in the Lord'. Paul does not so much pursue joy, rather he pursues Christ and resolutely focuses on him and his gospel, giving himself in the service of Christ and of Christ's people. He does this knowing that this is the way we experience true joy.

We see this with particular clarity as Philippians comes to its conclusion. As Paul thanks the church for their generous support, he says that what they give is 'credited' to their account (v 17). They are investing in gospel work and partnering closely with Paul. In a very real sense, they share the 'credit' for every sermon preached, every person saved, every church planted, every believer discipled. They are buying into a work which is offering great and eternal returns. Here are 'treasures in heaven', treasures that will last for ever.[3] The Philippians are not losing out through their sacrifice; far from it (vs 18,19). Rather, they are investing in the bank of heaven. Let's follow their example and speculate to accumulate!

Finance and festivity are not often thought of together, yet the connection is entirely appropriate. The investment Paul is talking about yields great dividends now, with many further returns to come. Where we spend our money reveals much about our true priorities. If someone reviewed our finances, what would they conclude was most important to us?

Review your financial giving and, if possible, commit to give more – cheerfully, as an investment for the future. Thank God for the joy which is – and will be – yours.

---

[1] Phil 3:1; 4:4 [2] John Newton, 1725–1807, 'Glorious Things of Thee are Spoken' [3] Matt 6:20

BIBLE IN A YEAR: Malachi 3,4; Revelation 22